D1001981

SPIRIT,
FAITH,
AND
CHURCH

BV
602
.P3
1970

The 1969 Walter and Mary Tuohy Chair Lectures

SPIRIT, FAITH, AND CHURCH

by
Wolfhart Pannenberg
Avery Dulles, S.J.
Carl E. Braaten

THE WESTMINSTER PRESS
Philadelphia

COPYRIGHT © MCMLXX THE WESTMINSTER PRESS

All rights reserved—no part of this book may be reproduced in any form without permission in writing from the publisher, except by a reviewer who wishes to quote brief passages in connection with a review in magazine or newspaper.

Scripture quotations from the Revised Standard Version of the Bible are copyright, 1946 and 1952, by the Division of Christian Education of the National Council of Churches, and are used by permission.

STANDARD BOOK NO. 664–20880–0

LIBRARY OF CONGRESS CATALOG CARD NO. 78–93000

BOOK DESIGN BY
DOROTHY ALDEN SMITH

Published by The Westminster Press ®
Philadelphia, Pennsylvania

PRINTED IN THE UNITED STATES OF AMERICA

BV
603
.P3

43377

CONTENTS

FOREWORD

DURING the recess between semesters in January, 1969, the Walter and Mary Tuohy Chair of Interreligious Studies at John Carroll University sponsored an intensive ten-day seminar entitled "Spirit—Faith—Church." The principal participants in this ecumenical and creative forum were Dr. Carl E. Braaten of the Lutheran School of Theology at Chicago, the Reverend Avery Dulles, S.J., of Woodstock College, and Dr. Wolfhart Pannenberg of the University of Munich.

Since its inception in 1967, the Tuohy Chair has sponsored the annual "Tuohy Lectures" at Kulas Auditorium, John Carroll University. During the midsemester seminar in 1969, six evening lectures were open to the general public. These six lectures, on Spirit, Faith, and Church, are the contents of this book.

I have arranged the lectures according to the general themes of Spirit, Faith, and Church. As might be expected in an ecumenical seminar, there are three chapters directly concerned with the church and only one on the working of the Spirit. Dr. Pannenberg's opening lecture on the

Spirit stimulated a fortnight of debate among seminar participants—and it will challenge those who read it today. In the second chapter, on authority and reason in faith, Father Dulles continues the penetrating study he began as professor of Fundamental Theology at Woodstock. Probably the most acclaimed lecture of the series was Dulles' incisive paper on doctrine and historical relativity—the third chapter of this book. Dulles brings to bear the insights of northern European theologians who have been struggling with this delicate problem and adds to their insights his own brilliant methodology. In chapters on the limits (and necessity) of pluralism and on ecclesiastical office, Dr. Braaten writes with the combination of theological depth and verbal articulateness American theologians have come to expect of him. Pannenberg concludes the series by offering to American readers the results of his impressive research on the future dimension in Christianity.

A unanimous impression of the hundred-plus participants in "Spirit—Faith—Church" was the surprising convergence among three leading theologians on essentials of Christian doctrine and structure. Differences were there, of course, but they were few and insignificant in comparison with the convergence of Braaten, Dulles, and Pannenberg on the large questions. In a brief foreword it is impossible to discuss or even mention the myriad areas of agreement which, in any case, the reader can see for himself in the following chapters. There are, however, six promising points of convergence that impressed me and which I single out here:

1. The seminar is permeated with an awareness of historicity. The perspective is modern and, therefore, historical. Revelation is seen as illuminating history and man's historicity. The individual biography in history assumes major importance and must be taken into account in any

reinterpretation of doctrine. Throughout these pages the authors are cautiously renewing doctrinal formulations from the historical perspective.

2. As might be expected in a seminar featuring Braaten and Pannenberg, there is emphasis on Christianity as a religion of the absolute future. Christ reveals the future of man, is the future of man, and points the church to the future Kingdom. Faith, hope, charity, apostolicity, catholicity, ecclesiastical office, doctrinal reformulation—all are seen in terms of that future hope which relativizes all particulars on behalf of the future and universal Kingdom of God.

3. Pluralism of doctrine, of rite, of structure is accepted and welcomed. In a historical perspective open to the absolute future there is room for pluralism in all areas of life and theology. Pluralism is recognized not only as desirable for the present, but as a past fact and future desirability. Today's theologies and structures, because they are in continuity with the past, are for that reason pluralistic with the past—and the future. Today's church, insofar as it is catholic, is for that very reason a church that is from its nature pluralist.

4. Although they rarely mention the fact, the authors propose a theology similar to the "political theology" current in the 1960s. A church that is historical, that welcomes secularization and pluralism, that relativizes all historical imperfections in hope of the future Kingdom is *political;* it creatively humanizes the city (the *polis*) of man on the active pilgrimage to the coming Kingdom which man himself must make.

5. The methodology is two-ended. That is, it looks to the apostolic past to safeguard Christian identity while reinterpreting doctrine for the present. While acting as servants to modern men and pointing toward the future Kingdom, these authors are respectful of history. Even

historically conditioned formulations and structures of the past—which were relevant and modern when the past was present—are respected because they preserve continuity with the past and because they help theologians reinterpret past formulations for a new present. Nothing previous is alien to historical man, not even past definitions framed in static categories against the background of an ontological self- and world-understanding.

6. Finally, the problem of doctrinal development permeates this book just as it does every ecumenical endeavor. We can visualize Father Dulles' late colleague, John Courtney Murray, standing majestically before a pre-conciliar audience at Yale and, as was his style, pointing prophetically to a future theological question. The basic theological question, Murray intoned, is not what you think of Christ or pope or church. The basic theological question is what you think of the *homoousian,* what you think of the development of dogma. These lectures attest to Murray's vision and I believe they augur a new and promising development in the development of dogma. The linear, organic view that has been so prevalent since Möhler and Newman is yielding to theories of doctrinal development based on historical self-understanding. It may be argued that a doctrine is apostolic not because it is an organic growth of the deposit, but is apostolic because different ages with different self-understandings proclaim the same apostolic faith. Historical reinterpretation, if it is to succeed, must be as courageous and as "liberal" as was the patristic reinterpretation of Christianity in Hellenic categories and as radical and challenging as was Aquinas' bold use of Aristotle in the thirteenth century. These lectures demonstrate that a historical view of doctrinal development, along with doctrinal "pruning" by all traditions, may lead to such convergence (within pluralism) that all Christians

may again be one even in allegiance to a pastoral Petrine office.

If SPIRIT, FAITH, AND CHURCH hastens in a small way the convergence of Christians, the generosity of the friends of Walter and Mary Tuohy and of John Carroll University will not have been in vain.

Edward P. Echlin, S.J.

John Carroll University

I

THE WORKING OF THE SPIRIT IN THE CREATION AND IN THE PEOPLE OF GOD

Wolfhart Pannenberg

IN the New Testament, Spirit is the name for the actual presence of divine reality in Christian experience and in the Christian community. Therefore, one might expect nothing to be more familiar to every Christian than the reality of the Spirit. But to the contrary, there is almost no other subject in modern theology so difficult to deal with as the doctrine of the Holy Spirit is. To begin with, it is rather hard to find out what kind of reality one is talking about in referring to the Holy Spirit. Many would say, it is the spirit of the Christian community. But what indication does the actual life of the Christian communities give for so fundamental a distinction from all other human communities as the exclusive presence of divine Spirit among Christians should be? Are not Christian communities very much like other human groups and associations? Do they differ from them in anything which could not be explained in terms of historical particularities? Is there any distinctive supernatural reality or mystery to be found in the empirical reality of the Christian churches? Similar questions can be asked in relation to individual Christian experience. All the dimensions of Christian religious life and experience including mysticism, prayer, and the occurrence of mysterious healing powers can be explained as examples of human religion and of a religious subjectivity without any reference to a reality that clearly and fundamentally separates Christian religious experience from all other human experience.

Thus one can hardly point to the Holy Spirit as to an obvious element in Christian individual experience or in the life of the Christian communities. The reality of the Holy Spirit is not to be identified by looking for elements that separate Christian experience and Christian community from all other human experience and community. Perhaps we have to try it the other way round by looking for the divine Spirit in what Christian experience and Christian community have in common with all other human experience and communities. Then the particular working of the Spirit in the people of God could be explained as a particular modification of what can be said of all human communities and of all human experience. This would correspond to the fact that in the Bible the divine spirit is understood as origin of all life, and this universal power is said to be present in the Christian community in a special way.

Thus we have to deal with the universal meaning of the spirit as origin of all life before turning to the particular presence of the spirit in the Christian community. The first task concerning the general function of the spirit has to start from a reflection upon the term "spirit," since there is no commonly accepted meaning of this word today. The discussion of the term will lead to a discussion of the reality indicated by the term, and then the question will arise, how the general meaning of spirit is to be related to the idea of a divine spirit. Is spirit in general something else than what we refer to as divine spirit? And if this is the case, how is that divine spirit to be related to spirit in general?

It is a well-known fact that in modern English the term "spirit" has been widely replaced by "mind." This is not necessarily to be taken as evidence of a preeminently intellectual conception of man, as Paul Tillich did.[1] The idea of mind even in the conception of John Locke included emotional elements of pleasure and pain.[2] And in recent literature it has been emphasized by Gilbert Ryle that the concept of mind is not to be limited to intellectual processes.[3] The loss of the term "spirit" in anthropology needs another explanation. It seems to be related to the connotation of spirit as an immaterial substance. John Locke, while attributing all material operations to the mind, still felt the need to explain those operations as "actions of some other substance"—in distinction from the body; and with reference to that immaterial substance behind our mental operations he used the term "spirit." [4] David Hume, however, eliminated the idea of substance; and therefore he had no further use for the term "spirit" in his *Treatise of Human Nature.* He continued to speak of the mind and of operations of the mind, but he said: "The mind is not a substance in which the perceptions inhere. They compose the mind, not belong to it." [5] Perhaps this explains the fading of the term "spirit" in the philosophical discussion of human nature. The term "spirit" suggested that the mind had to be conceived of as immaterial substance, and this idea was avoided by the suppression of the term "spirit." In this connection, it is interesting that Hegel's *Phänomenologie des Geistes* was translated into English *Phenomenology of the Mind,* not Phenomenology of the Spirit. Certainly Hegel did not mean by *Geist* an immaterial substance. But on the other hand, his term *Geist* had a broader meaning than "mind," especially because *Geist* transcends the individual and refers to a universal truth which is embodied in the society, in the state, and only shared by the individuals. Edmund W. Sinnott, in his book *The Biology of the Spirit* (1955), has made an interesting attempt to reintroduce the term "spirit" into a biological description of human nature. He emphasizes that reason being the "latest development of mind" [6] represents only one side of human nature. On the other side, there are "deep-seated inborn urgencies and desires, arising spontaneously in the mind but subject to a wide measure of direction, often dragging man down to the level of the beasts but coming to flower as the highest expression of what he is and what he might become." These "deep-seated inborn urgencies and desires" he called "the human spirit." [7]

This idea of spirit does not entail the assumption of an immaterial substance but refers to the irrational elements in human nature. Spirit as understood by Sinnott may be called with a phrase of Paul Tillich "a dimension of life." And as Tillich's language does, the connection of spirit with life in the precise sense of biology reminds us of the way the Hebrew Bible spoke of the divine Spirit as the origin of all life.

But while Sinnott takes spirit as a function of the living organism, the Bible understood life as a function of the spirit. In the Biblical conception the spirit differs from the organic structure, although it is the spirit who gives life to the organism. Thus the spirit is not just the human spirit, but closely connected with God. The human spirit is only a participation of the divine spirit. Hence in Genesis the human body comes to life only when God "breathed into his nostrils the breath of life" (Gen. 2:7). And when God takes away the breath of life, his creatures die.

Thus Psalm 104 addresses God with reference to his creatures: "When thou hidest thy face, they are dismayed;

when thou takest away their breath, they die and return to their dust. When thou sendest forth thy Spirit, they are created; and thou renewest the face of the ground" (vs. 29 f.). Here the same Hebrew word *ruah* is used to denote the breath of the creatures and the spirit of God. And as the last phrase of the quotation identifies the divine spirit with those prolific winds that renew the surface of the ground in springtime, in the same way the prophet Ezekiel in a great vision saw the dry and dead bones of his people come to life again when the divine wind breathed the spirit of life into them (Ezek. 37:5 ff.). This spirit is not identical with the idea of the soul as spiritual substance apart from the body. The spirit is not the individual man, but the divine power that makes the individual man alive. The human spirit is not an independent reality of its own, but a mere participation of the divine spirit, and a passing one.

Is there any analogy in our modern understanding of life to this idea of life as related to a reality which transcends the living organism and yet quickens and animates it? Modern biology describes life as a self-creative reality incorporated in the living cell. Generally, one doesn't look for a transcendent principle of life. And yet, life can be interpreted as ecstatic. I take this suggestion from Paul Tillich, although Tillich himself uses the idea of ecstasy for his basic description of spiritual presence, i.e., of the *divine* spirit grasping the human person, but remaining distinct from the human spirit, from spirit as a dimension of life.[8] I venture to disregard this careful distinction and to dismiss it as an artificial one. Does not the element of ecstasy belong to the phenomenon of the human spirit? Doesn't it penetrate all spiritual activities of man? Isn't the experience of the artist an ecstatic one, an experience of elevation, of being elevated beyond himself? Isn't every discovery of a truth which is valid not only for oneself, but also for other people, an ecstatic experience, elevating the individual beyond his individual particularity? Isn't the same true of every act of freedom when we become free from what we have been so far? Modern anthropology conceives of man as a self-transcending being. As early as man experiences something else as something else he is reaching beyond himself. The literal meaning of the term "ecstatic" is precisely this—to get beyond oneself; and this now seems to emerge as a basic structural element of human life.

But not only of *human* life: every living organism lives beyond itself, for every organism needs an appropriate environment for the activity of its life. When kept in isolation, no organism is fit for life. Hence every organism lives beyond itself. A particular aspect of this ecstatic character of life is to be found in its relation to time: every organism relates itself to a future that will change its present conditions. This is evident in the drives and urgencies of life, but also in negative anticipations such as fear and horror.

Perhaps the human mind can be described as a special realization of this ecstatic character of life. Man not only lives beyond himself in having experience of what is going on in his environment and relevant for his own life, but the human mind is characterized by a reflective attitude to himself and is therefore able to take his stand beyond himself and to know that. The human mind represents an intensified form of self-transcendence, i.e., of the ecstatic structure of life. The experience of freedom, the capability for abstract cognition, the particular ecstasy of imaginative inspiration—all this seems closely related to the distinctive structure of the mind, to his reflective nature, to his ability to look at himself from a distance and therefore to take the position of something else in distinction from himself. This ecstatic element of the life of the mind I call "spirit."

It is at work in the ecstatic activity of all life, but only the human mind participates subjectively in the spirit since the mind is able to take his stand beyond himself, to have his center outside himself.

In this connection one consequence of the reflective self-transcendence of man is extremely important: in taking a stand beyond himself, the human mind is no longer himself the unity of his experience, but is looking for something beyond himself that gives unity to his experiences. We experience the particular only within a wider horizon of meaning which is anticipated as some sort of unity.[9] This underlies all processes of abstractive thinking. But the unity beyond the individual is also concrete in form of a community of individuals. Hence in the reflective consciousness of man the importance of social life for the individual develops to a new level: the social community in its difference from individual existence becomes constitutive for the individual's experience of the unity and identity of his existence.[10] On the other hand, however, the human mind can reflect upon the limitations of the unifying validity of given ideas as well as of established social systems, and thus the individual conceives the unity of reality and meaning that constitutes his own existence, beyond the limitations of particular concepts of universal truth as well as beyond the limitations of a particular society.

The unity beyond and constituting individual existence is not yet definitely revealed, but is at the same time presupposed in every act of existence. Because human existence presupposes that unity, we take as basis of our individual lives the provisional appearances of that unity in social institutions and in certain ideas. These function as the universal basis of existence, although at the same time that basic unity can still be questioned.

The spiritual unity beyond but constituting individual

existence is perhaps best explained by the idea of truth. Truth implies unity of experience, therefore excludes contradiction. Further, truth in two ways transcends the individual, first as unity of individual and environment, because truth requires a correspondence and conformity of subject and object; secondly, as unity of the individual subject with other subjects, since something can be true for me only on the condition that it is true for others also.

The spiritual dimension is not identical with the human mind, since only in some sort of ecstasy, only in getting beyond himself, the human mind participates in truth, receives the inspiration of beauty, and obtains freedom. While the mind belongs to the natural endowment of a human being, he does not always and not automatically succeed in spiritual achievements.

Spirit is at the same time transcendent and immanent in man: imminent, because only the spirit grants personal identity and fulfillment to human life. When we speak of the spirit of a man or of an action or of an institution, we point to the principle vitalizing the man or the action or the institution, each regarded as a whole in itself. On the other hand, this unity in spirit is immanent in a man or in a social group only insofar as they transcend themselves. To speak of the spirit of a man or a group or an action is to characterize them by an ecstatic unity that integrates the life of the individual or the group. In this respect it may be helpful to contrast spirit with mood. A mood is never ecstatic. When a person is in a certain mood, this certainly characterizes the person in his totality, if only for some time. Mood refers to "the frame of mind" of a person.[11] But as such a mood belongs to the given situation of a person, it has no liberating power as spirit has which also concerns the totality of a person, but in relation to his self-transcendent activity. There is, however, a point of contact between mood and spirit. In a cheerful mood, man is in disposition for being grasped by the action of the spirit. On the other hand, in a depressed mood man is not, to be sure, out of every contact with the spirit, but he is, as we say, in low spirits. Still different is the case when one speaks of a man as being in bad spirits. Here the human participation in spirit is dominated by non-spiritual factors, but in such a way that an analogy develops to genuine spiritual ecstasy, except in the liberating effect of the latter. Such is the phenomenon referred to as obsession.

The element of transcendence in spirit suggests that after all it might be neither necessary nor wise to admit a fundamental distinction between a human spirit and a divine spirit. The ecstatic, self-transcendent character of all spiritual experience brings sufficiently to bear the transcendence of God over against all created beings. The spirit never belongs in a strict sense to the creature in his immanent nature, but the creature participates in the spirit —and I venture to say: in the divine spirit—by transcending itself, i.e., by being elevated beyond itself in the ecstatic experience that illustrates the working of the spirit. We remember: the spirit is not the mind, but the human mind comes to life only when he is touched by the spirit. And the same seems to be true of all living creatures.

Thus the idea of spirit allows us to do justice to the transcendence of God and at the same time to explain his immanence in his creation. Theology loses this chance when a fundamental distinction is accepted between divine and human spirit. Therefore, such a distinction doesn't seem wise. It would only duplicate what we experience. It would deprive the divine spirit of any intelligible function in our understanding of reality and, especially, of life, while human spirituality would be taken as immanent in the human nature and thus lose its distinctive ecstatic character. The strongest reason, on the other hand, to adopt that distinction was to secure the divine transcendence. But this argument can arise only when the ecstatic character of human spiritual experience is mistaken for something that belongs to the natural equipment of men. Of course, human experience, even in its ecstatic self-transcendence, does not perceive the divine spirit, but only participates in some way in his action. Therefore, the action of the spirit can be received in perverted ways, the most extreme of which is known as possession or obsession. Without the working of the divine spirit the self-transcendent activity of life and thus life itself must pale, but the "breath" of the spirit does not necessarily exclude the ambiguities of life precisely in the process of its self-transcendence. Tillich has given a penetrating description of these ambiguities. On the human level, they can be summarized in the following way: on the one hand, man can become himself only in reaching beyond himself, in self-abnegation. But on the other hand, in being elevated beyond himself, he may still be concerned only for himself.

Because in every new situation, in every new possibility of his life, man is continuing his old self, the entire history of his life can be dominated by a tendency to persist in what one always was and to take every new situation just as another opportunity to hold one's ground. Thus personal identity remains ambiguous. It can remain within the circle of the personal past in spite of the self-transcendence of spiritual experience. It can even result from demonic obsession. In both cases, to be sure, no truly comprehensive personal identity, but only the appearance of it can develop, since the fundamental relatedness of human life to a future beyond itself is suppressed or distorted. True personal identity emerges only through a series of ecstatic events or spiritual experience, integrating all the different aspects of an individual's life. But even in this case a provisional form of spiritual unity is often mistaken as definite, or the true meaning of a situation is missed, or faith and hope are fixed on narrow and, in the final analysis, shaky objectives. All these ambiguities of self-identity in self-transcendence can be traced back to the fact that in the present form of human life there is no pre-established harmony between the spirit and the personal self. Again and again the personal self separates itself from the spirit and therefore man must transcend himself in order to find himself. The separation between the empirical self and the spirit again and again separates man from the future of life and exposes his personal life to death.

At this point it becomes possible to characterize the special form of spiritual presence in the Christian community. While the spirit is working in all life as the vitalizing principle, the lure to self-transcendence and as the inspirative power of ecstasy—the Christian community lives on the basis of the message of a new life, which is no longer separated from the spiritual origin of all life. In early Christianity, the Pauline epistles almost identified the new life originated in the resurrection of Christ with the reality of the divine spirit. Therefore Paul described that new life as a *soma pneumatikon*, a spiritual body. In contrast to the old life this new one will remain in unity with the origin of life and therefore never perish. And because the Christian proclamation transmits the message of the new life, it is itself spiritual and communicates spirit and joy. The Christian message is accepted in ecstatic acts of faith, love, and hope. In faith man relies completely on a reality other than himself, on the new life which has been revealed in Christ. The Christian understanding of love has the particularity that love is seen as creative, and man has to be elevated beyond his narrow perspective of self-interest in order to participate in the creativity of love. That elevation beyond himself is accomplished in faith which—if genuine—should liberate man from narrow-mindedness, and in hope which opens up the promise of life not only for oneself but for all mankind, thus inspiring the creativity of love.

It is obvious that the average reality of Christian life and Christian communities is not altogether convincing if compared with the full dynamic of the New Testament description of Spiritual Presence in faith, love, and hope. Obviously even these basic forms of spiritual presence are not simply immune against the ambiguities of life. They can be, and very often they are badly distorted. The most pressing problem in this field is without any question the weakness and inefficiency of Christian love. There is grow-ing impatience in the world expressed in criticism of the Christian proclamation because, after all, two thousand years of Christian history didn't change so much the human condition, the sufferings of human beings. Christians seem to be rather complacent people. They have their popula-tion centers in the richest countries of this world, but they don't manage to change the miserable living conditions of the majority of mankind, but rather contribute to, con-tinue, perpetuate, or even aggravate the disastrous occur-rences of hunger, war, and political or economical aliena-tion.

Obviously, the ecstatic power of the spirit and, especially, of love elevating man beyond the limitations of the con-ditions in his natural and social environment and in him-self, is weaker than one should expect on the basis of the New Testament assurances concerning the presence of the Spirit in the Christian community. As Christians, we may deplore this fact. But, as things are, mere moralistic criti-cism of the weakness of Christian love seems insufficient and, again, inefficient. One has to look at the reasons for this phenomenon. Then, one may conclude, it is the private conception of Christian love that makes it largely ineffi-

4 3 3 7 7

cient today. But to become fully aware of what this means, one has to take into account the distortions of faith and hope as well. For these represent the motivation of Christian love, and if the latter is weak and the spirit cannot get through the channels of human action, the clot may well be in the conception of faith or hope. Especially faith only too often narrows the outlook of the Christian instead of broadening it. It still seems to be an exception rather than the rule among Christians that faith means the awakening to freedom, to a new vision of human life. Instead, faith is still, and preeminently, understood as acceptance of a number of rather strange propositions which have little to do with the realities of everyday life in the modern world. Underlying all this is what I want to call the dogmatic distorture of faith.

Few Christians are aware of the consequences of the fact that faith, above all, is trust uniting a person with Jesus and that the power of this faith is beyond comprehension. The consequences are that the authenticity of faith is not necessarily impaired by the limitations of understanding. Although of course some understanding is always involved, faith can be true and effective even if the understanding which it is connected with is largely wrong. Dogmatic formulas cannot be, by themselves, a criterion for whether the faith of a person is genuine or not. Although it belongs to the task of theological reflection to ask for the conditions of genuine faith, neither that reflection itself nor any result of it is constitutive for faith, and everybody knows that theological questions remain always controversial if they are not silenced by some kind of nonspiritual power. Faith, however, can and should be one, notwithstanding different theologies and conflicting dogmatic propositions. The pluralism of doctrinal positions is, indeed, a condition and a test of the freedom of faith.

Since the Christian church is a community of faith and

not of doctrine, there is no sufficient reason why any differences in opinion or doctrine automatically should prevent the unity in faith and spirit. Of course, the unity in
spirit must have some way to manifest itself. Without any
such manifestation there can be no unity nor consciousness
of it. But the spiritual unity need not manifest itself in any
uniform proposition of doctrine. The sensibility of this
generation concerning the historical relativity of doctrinal
formulations should pave the way for the insight that
genuine agreement on one uniform doctrine is a rare exception even among people who believe themselves united
in the same spirit.

Certainly, agreement in questions of doctrine remains to
be desired. But in the provisional situation of man in the
dynamics of an ongoing historical process it must be an
exception and should no longer be made a condition of
unity in faith. This is constituted by the intention to have
community with Jesus, and it is to be recognized even in
those people who without knowing about their relation to
Jesus intend what Jesus stood for. In some cases, to be
sure, doctrinal differences may be one factor in a division
of faith. But to decide about unity or disunity in faith is
always a pastoral decision, not simply a doctrinal one; and
the performance of pastoral action is subject to the judgment of those who share the same spirit, who authorize the
holder of a pastoral office in a Christian community.

The dogmatic distortion of faith is related to a corre-
sponding distortion of the pastoral office in the church,
which often has been influenced by a dogmatic and legalistic rigidity resulting in intolerant uniformity within the
Christian community as well as in relation to others and
to secular institutions. It was a dogmatic spirit that pro-
duced most of the divisions in Christian history. Perhaps
in former times it was difficult to avoid dogmatic uniformity, if the identity of the Christian tradition was to be pre-

served. But at least in modern times the continuous historical quest for the original and genuine character of the Christian faith, controversial though the results may remain, has developed new instruments of testing the identity of contemporary Christian faith with the Christian origins. If there was some justification for dogmatic uniformity in former periods of Christian history, there is no need for it any longer. The Christian faith must overcome its distortion by intolerance—be it in praxis or only in principle—and by the narrow-minded presumption of being in secure and definite possession of the truth. Such a mentality, of course, could not fail to weaken the impulse of love or even to mistake the fanaticism in spreading one's own opinions or form of life for an act of love in itself.

Besides the dogmatic distortion of faith there is the escapist distortion. The temptation of escapism arises from the fact that the ultimate reality of the new life in Christ creates a distance to everything that is but a provisional, passing reality. This distance inherent in the Christian faith over against the given world can release an activity which in the light of the ultimate future intends to change the given conditions of life; they need no longer be accepted as permanently valid. More often in Christian history, however, the distance of the Christian faith from the provisional reality in the world has induced Christians to turn their backs to the world and "seek God alone."

Presumably, the dogmatic illusion of being in possession of the definite truth of the divine revelation in the definite, unchangeable form of the dogma added to the temptation of leaving the provisional reality of the present world to itself. It allowed for the illusion, as if the truth of the divine revelation was not involved in this passing, provisional world. In this form the Christian faith involuntarily performed the ideological function of perpetuating the given structures of life, especially in the society. In this form the Christian faith could not, except in a rather limited way, become the motivation for the dynamics of love that intends to change the sufferings and iniquities of men due to the given conditions of human life. But the God of the incarnation is a God who did not avoid getting involved in the present world. The Christian faith is distorted by the escapist attitude which has been so influential in Christian history.

Closely connected with the two distortions of the Christian faith there has occurred a distortion of Christian hope: the Christian hope was affected by the escapist distortion of the faith, when it was related exclusively to the world to come, when Christians were not aware that the future of salvation has already begun in the history of Jesus and should continue to come through, although still in provisional ways, in this suffering world. In addition, the Christian hope was preeminently understood as hope for the correct believer, but somewhat less as universal hope for all mankind as it was revealed in the new life of Christ. Thus the Christian hope has often been more or less restricted to the private concern of the believer for himself. In this form, however, it could not become an impulse for the universality of Christian love.

Genuine Christian hope means a fascinating vision of a new life for all mankind, even for the natural world, and it is meant to influence as much as possible the miserable and sometimes horrible conditions of present human life not only for some individuals, but also for entire societies and for all humanity. It is only this comprehensive humanistic vision which opens up the universal perspective for the creative activity of Christian love.

But how can the individual Christian really get to work within this universal perspective? This is hardly possible without the Christian community. It requires a renewal of the Christian church. The association of all

Christians is needed in order to manifest the universal meaning of Christian hope and, especially, to articulate and bring to bear the universal intention of Christian love. In the present situation it is a question whether such a move can reasonably be expected from the established hierarchies and power structures of the confessional churches and denominations. If so, it will be most welcome. But in all those established institutions there are strong tendencies to give priority to the preservation of traditional particularities over the urgent needs and possibilities of the time. Therefore, Christians must not wait until their superiors get moving or until the theologians arrive at definite solutions of disputes about doctrine. Every Christian, learned or not, has a share through his faith in Christ in the divine spirit and this with the promise of being permanently endowed with the spirit. Although he participates in the Spirit through the ministry of the church, he is now immediately united with the spirit and authorized to judge everything. The modern idea of autonomy and the slogan of "universal priesthood" in the Reformation have their common root here. This spiritual autonomy authorizes the individual Christian layman to judge the Christian adequacy of everything that happens in the church, especially the spiritual adequacy of the way ecclesiastical offices are administered. Therefore every Christian is authorized to participate in the spiritual renewal of the church.

In our days there is a widespread feeling among Christians that the traditional divisions of denominations and confessional churches do not prevent spiritual unity with their fellow Christians who come from different traditions. This feeling doesn't reveal incompetence in theological matters, but rather a sound spiritual judgment. Those Christians should associate themselves in order to urge their theologians and officials to accelerate their preparations for Christian reunification. There is no divine privilege for theologians and officials to indefinitely extend their considerations and hesitations before the average Christian might be allowed to live according to his confession in one universal church. This does not deny the importance of theology, nor that of ecclesiastical office. Especially the latter may prove to be an indispensable sign and instrument of unity. The unity of a new universal church may even need its manifestation in a single highest office. There is no necessary mutual exclusion between spirit and office. But the united universal church of the future is not possible on the basis of a uniform doctrine, nor on the basis of a superiority of its offices beyond all criticism. The spirit judges everything, and the spirit is granted to every individual Christian. By the working of this spirit a new Christian unity is emerging in our time, a new universal church: it will be one without being uniform, and thus it may become a model for the human dream of a liberal and tolerant pluriformity without surrender of unity. The new universal church must change the authoritarian structures of traditional concepts of hierarchical order, without being deprived of the service of a pastoral office working on all levels of ecclesiastical administration. Thus the Christian community might become a model for the human dream to surpass the conflicts between those who impose their rule and those who are expected to obey.

NOTES

1. Paul Tillich, *Systematic Theology* (The University of Chicago Press, 1963), Vol. III, pp. 21 f.
2. John Locke, *An Essay Concerning Human Understanding* II, 20, 1 ff.

3. Gilbert Ryle, *The Concept of Mind* (1st published, 1949; University Paperbacks, No. 8, Barnes & Noble, Inc., 1966), pp. 26 f.

4. Locke, *Essay* II, 23, 5.

5. David Hume, *An Inquiry Concerning Human Understanding*, Appendix II.

6. Edmund W. Sinnott, *The Biology of the Spirit* (1st published, 1955; The Viking Press, Compass Books, No. 17), p. 126.

7. *Ibid.*, p. 127.

8. Tillich, *op. cit.*, pp. 112, 114 ff.

9. Cf. Karl Rahner, *Hörer des Wortes*, neubearb. von J. B. Metz (Munich: Kösel-Verlag, 1963), pp. 77 ff., and also *Geist in Welt zur Metaphysik der endlichen Erkenntnis bei Thomas von Aquin* (3d ed., 1964), pp. 129 ff.

10. George H. Mead, *Mind, Self and Society* (The University of Chicago Press, 1934), pp. 82 ff.

11. Ryle, *op. cit.*, pp. 99 f.; cf. p. 100: Mood words characterize "the total 'set' of a person" during the short period of their application.

II

AUTHORITY AND REASON IN THE ASSENT OF FAITH

Avery Dulles, S.J.

IT IS NOT my purpose in this paper to inquire whether or not the assent of Christian faith can be justified at the bar of reason. My aim is not apologetic. I shall assume that there are Christians and that they accept certain things as a matter of religious faith. This being granted, I should like to raise the question to what extent assents of this character rest upon reason and to what extent upon authority.

Distinguished authors such as Étienne Gilson[1] and H. Richard Niebuhr[2] have lucidly set forth the various ways in which the relations between faith and reason have been conceived in different theological schools. I shall not repeat their analyses here, except to note that there are a number of typical schematizations. Some so stress the opposition that they conclude that one must either accept faith at the expense of reason, or renounce faith in order to follow the demands of reason. Others, impressed by the harmony between faith and reason, assert that they support one another or even that they are two different routes to the same goal. A third position would situate faith and reason in two different spheres, and would consequently deny the possibility of any genuine conflict or mutual confirmation. This school would say that faith gives one type of truth, reason another, and that there can be no overlapping, provided only that each remains in its proper sphere.

The position one adopts in this debate will depend in great measure on how one conceives the meaning of the terms "faith" and "reason." Most of us unconsciously presuppose certain conceptions derived from a long tradition which may not be a wholly good one. Since the Middle Ages it has become common, perhaps especially in Roman Catholicism but also in other Christian traditions, to hold that faith-knowledge is based on authority, whereas rational knowledge is that which is or can be acquired by scientific investigation. Thus the problem of the relations between faith and reason is connected with that of the relations between authority and science. In order to throw light upon the first problem, I shall have to make some remarks on the second.

A typical representative of the view prevalent since the Middle Ages is Blaise Pascal, who formulates the contrast between faith and science as follows:

If it is desired to know who was the first king of the French; at what point geographers place the first meridian; what words were commonly used in a dead language, or anything else of this sort, what other means than books can give us what we want? And who could possibly add anything to what they tell us, since we wish only to know what they contain?

Authority alone can enlighten us in these matters. But such authority has its principal force in theology, because there it is inseparable from truth, and truth is unobtainable in any other way. Thus, to give complete certitude concerning matters most incomprehensible to reason, it is sufficient to show that they are found in the sacred books; and to demonstrate the uncertainty of things which seem quite evident, it is enough to point out that they are not contained in Scripture. For the principles of theology are above both nature and reason. Since the mind of man is too feeble to attain them by its own efforts, it cannot achieve such lofty understanding unless it is borne by an almighty and supernatural force. But in matters which lie within the scope of the senses and of reason, the situation is far different. Here authority is useless; reason alone is in a position to know them. The two types of knowledge have their separate prerogatives. In the former area authority had all the advantage; here reason reigns in its turn.[3]

On this theory, theology is in effect reduced to history; that is, to the writings of human witnesses who were in a position to record God's revelations. History, in turn, is treated as a discipline in which criticism can hold no place; one simply has to accept the statements of the witnesses or else resign oneself to ignorance. Thus religious knowledge is made abjectly dependent on authority, and authority is depicted in extrinsic terms.

We live in an age when, for better or for worse, extrinsic authority is mistrusted; and if theology can do nothing but reason from authority, theology will be dismissed as a sterile pursuit. The reasons for the modern distrust of authority are many, and would include considerations such as these:

1. Authority is felt to be a threat to vitality. What is proper to life is immanent action—i.e., action that begins spontaneously from within the subject and leads to self-fulfillment. Authority—in the sense explained above—acts upon a man from outside, and he is largely passive with respect to it.

2. Authority seems to be pitted against freedom. The more finality is claimed for authority, the less room is left for free choice and creativity. A man is at least morally

constrained to accept what is presented to him, rather than to follow his own judgment.

3. Authority is suspected of being inimical to truth. In any society the ruling authorities are tempted to suppress inquiry or criticism in order to protect their own position and to avoid questioning of their own competence. Contemporary man has reason to suspect that where there is a lack of free inquiry, criticism, and debate, truth is likely to be suppressed. One of Charles Davis' principal charges against the Roman Catholic Church is what he calls its concern for authority at the expense of truth.[4]

4. In our contemporary democratic society, authority runs against the grain because it erects a privileged class who are held to have primary access to the sources of wisdom. In Christianity the ordinary believer is in danger of being reduced to the status of a second-class citizen in comparison with the authorized interpreters of the tradition or of Scripture.

5. When the decisive authority is that of witnesses from the past, there arises the further difficulty that true progress seems to be impossible. Modern man is rarely content to do what could equally well have been done, and was perhaps better done, by his ancestors. He does not feel that his own experiences and reflections should be dismissed as insignificant.

These difficulties against authority in religion and in faith may prove nothing more than the pride and insubordination of modern man. But before we rebuke the times in which we live we should look closely to see whether there is a true incompatibility between Christianity and the modern *Zeitgeist*. If we turn to the New Testament, we can find good grounds for thinking that Christianity was originally heralded as a way of gaining fullness of life, freedom, truth, human equality, and

progress. According to John 10:10, Jesus came in order
that we might have life, and have it more abundantly.
Repeatedly in the New Testament, truth and freedom are
stressed as central Christian values (e.g., John 8:32; Gal.
5:1). The Bible, too, makes much of the immediate relationship between each individual believer and the Holy
Spirit (e.g., John 6:45; I John 2:27) and hence permits no
total subjection of one man to another. Further, the New
Testament intimates the possibility of future progress
within the Christian community. For example, it promises
that the Holy Spirit will lead Christians into all truth, and
will teach them what the disciples were not in a position
to hear from the lips of Jesus (John 16:12–13). Thus the
Christian sources themselves suggest the inadequacy of
presenting Christian faith as a passive submission to what
human authorities hand down to us from the past.

Pascal's statement that the principles of faith lie beyond
the limits of both nature and reason is scarcely applicable
to Christianity as it existed in New Testament times. Even
those mysteries which modern theology usually places altogether beyond the scope of reason—such as the incarnation
and the Trinity—were learned by reflection on the data of
experience. If the early community accepted Jesus as Mes-
siah and Lord, this was not so much because he explicitly
claimed these titles for himself (very likely he did not) as
because his entire ministry and career—as apprehended by
the disciples—could not be accounted for on any other
supposition. So, too, the doctrine of the Holy Spirit, the
third person of the Trinity, was gradually built up in the
light of the experiences of the early community, including
the extraordinary charisms that came upon the church
after Pentecost. The early preaching of the apostles did
not take the form of heralding a strange set of historical
facts, but rather that of a commentary on well-known
public events—such as miraculous healings, glossolalia,

persecutions, conversions, etc. Faith and reason supported one another to the extent that they did not actually coincide. Faith aimed to give a coherent grasp of the facts that clamored for explanation.

While many of us would wish that in our time we might see palpable facts demanding the Christian message as their only suitable explanation, we can hardly claim that this is the case. It is probably inevitable that the most basic elements of salvation history now have to be culled from the past, out of ancient documents. But this situation does not constrain us to flee to the blind authoritarianism advocated by Pascal. Augustine and the medieval Augustinian tradition provide a view of the relationship between faith and reason more congenial to the modern mind. Augustine holds that while one must begin by accepting certain facts on the authority of apparently reliable witnesses, faith should not be content to remain a matter of hearsay; it should lead on to understanding. "Unless you believe," he repeatedly affirms, "you shall not understand." [5] Anselm's formula, *fides quaerens intellectum,* faithful to the Augustinian tradition, indicates that the truths of faith may prove their value by their power to illuminate experience.

Historically the modern split between faith and reason is closely connected with the revival of Aristotelianism. In the view of Aristotle and his Christian disciples, most notably Thomas Aquinas, reason had to do with what could be established by science, i.e., by demonstrative argument from self-evident principles. Obviously the truths of the Christian faith could not be vindicated in this way. Against the efforts of some rationalists to reduce faith to deductive reasoning of this kind, Thomistic theology affirmed that faith went beyond the scope of reason. Thus the impression gained ground that faith was a leap which, if not wild and irrational, at least went beyond the evidence. In some later Scholastic treatments, both Catholic and Protestant, the contents of faith took on the aspect of a foreign body of knowledge piped down from heaven. Prior to faith, reason could no doubt give extrinsic grounds for accepting the testimony of the divine witnesses. After the act of faith had been made, reason could deduce consequences. But the premises of faith—the articles of the creed and the affirmations of Scripture—had to be accepted by submission to authority, and hence without intrinsic grounds.

As a result of radical changes taking place in the self-understanding of both science and theology, the traditional opposition between scientific reason and theology is rapidly breaking down. For one thing, science is no longer thought to rest upon self-evident principles, or to proceed by stringent demonstration, or to seek only universal, necessary, and immutable truths. It deals readily with particular facts, with the process of change, and with probabilities. It extends not only to the mathematical and physical realms but to human affairs, including psychology, sociology, and religion.

In particular, the opposition between science and history, so fundamental to the outlook of Pascal, has evanesced. No self-respecting historian considers himself abjectly dependent on what his sources state. He appraises the sources in view of the opportunity the authors might have had to verify the alleged facts, the likelihood of confusion, bias, fraud, etc. Then he reconstructs the events with due allowance for distortions that may have crept into the record. Since the time of Pascal, a critical approach to the Christian sources, including the Scriptures, has been accepted by most churches, and this acceptance has drastically altered the relationship between faith and reason.

Further, as Bernard Lonergan has recently noted, theology has ceased to be the kind of deductive science that it was thought to be in the age of high Scholasticism. "It has become an empirical science in the sense that Scripture and Tradition now supply not premises, but data. The data has to be viewed in its historical perspective. It has to be interpreted in the light of contemporary techniques and procedures." [6] The modern theologian is not content to quote statements from Scripture or from the documents of tradition. He feels obliged to evaluate these, taking account of the historical stresses and strains that may have influenced the statements in question, and asking to what extent the statements would have to be reformulated in order to be suitable expressions of Christian faith in the circumstances of our day.

As a result of the changes that have taken place, I believe that it is no longer useful to set up a contrast between faith on the one hand and science on the other. As a kind of thesis I should like to propose that there is a basic similarity of structure in man's progress toward knowledge in the scientific and religious spheres. In every human discipline both authority and personal insight play a role —though the types of authority and insight, and their respective proportions, vary according to the nature of the subject matter in each particular case.

To clarify the thesis just proposed it will be helpful to distinguish between two aspects of knowledge in any field —whether secular or religious. The first is learning, the acquisition of what has already been achieved by others; the second, discovery, by which we mean a more original conquest of the mind. In each of these two areas faith has a place, but the concept of faith is somewhat different.

In the learning process, it is always necessary to rely heavily on the authority of predecessors. Michael Polanyi points out how essential is this reliance even in the secular sciences:

The assimilation of great systems of articulate lore by novices of various grades is made possible by a previous act of affiliation, by which the novice accepts the apprenticeship to a community which cultivates this lore, appreciates its values, and strives to act by its standards. This affiliation begins with the fact that a child submits to education within a community, and it is confirmed throughout life to the extent to which the adult continues to place exceptional confidence in the intellectual leaders of the same community.[7]

What Polanyi here says of the scientific community is applicable a fortiori to a community of religious faith. If an individual wishes to expose himself to the full impact of the highest religious insights that have been attained in a given tradition, he must affiliate with the group, accept apprenticeship within the community, and place his trust in its religious leaders. If I wish to understand yoga I must live under the tutelage of a yogi; if I wish to understand Christianity I must join the Christian community and gradually become initiated into its mysteries. The meaning of religious rites and doctrines simply cannot be understood by an outsider, a mere spectator. Only if I am willing to contemplate life through the eyes of believers, can I discover whether the vision of faith is helpful and acceptable to me. This quasi-experimental kind of commitment appears to correspond with what Augustine advocated in his celebrated formula, "Unless you believe you shall not understand."

It may be objected, of course, that submission to education within a group—with all the confidence in the group that this implies—will limit the individual's possibilities of making an original contribution. Of course there is such a thing as a mechanical and passive submission to authority, which never passes on to the stage of active appropriation and understanding. But normally speaking, education aims to put a man in a position in which he achieves insights that would otherwise lie beyond his capacity. In this sense it enhances rather than restricts the originality of the individual.

In all human traditions, the transmission of knowledge and skills involves a constant process of revision. This is evident even in the field of language. As words are used in new contexts, the previous usage is continually being modified. So, too, when we agree with someone else's opinion we almost inevitably modify his thought, no matter how slightly. My assent cannot be a perfect carbon copy of yours. And conversely, there is no such thing as total dissent. The sharpest disagreement includes a partial submission to an existing consensus. Even the most radical revolutionary appeals to certain principles accepted within the society he is trying to revolutionize.

This dialectic of continuity and innovation, which is at work in all human acceptance of authority, plays an important part in the history of religion. Great disciples have never been content to repeat verbatim the lessons of their masters, but rather to go forward in their footsteps. As we know from history, the major innovators in Christianity have always been men deeply steeped in their religious tradition—men who drew from the tradition the weapons by which they fought against the existing forms of church life. This is evident in the case of Roman Catholic reformers such as Bernard of Clairvaux, Francis of Assisi, and Ignatius Loyola, as well as among Protestants such as Luther, Calvin, and Kierkegaard.

The Christian tradition makes room for creative criticism of itself, for it teaches that human sinfulness, as well as the grace of the Holy Spirit, is at work in the entire history of the church. Sinfulness, of course, is at work in the religious revolutionary too: and he must seriously ask himself whether he has been sufficiently attentive to what the tradition might have to say to him. Paradoxically, it is only a thorough immersion in the Christian tradition that puts one in a position to bring an authentically Christian criticism to bear against it.

The learning process, therefore, both in religion and in other disciplines, involves at least a provisional and to some extent critical submission to authority. In Christianity the submission can never be absolute because a man can never transfer to anyone else the responsibility for his own religious faith. That must be a matter between himself and God. Nobody's faith can be an exact replica of someone else's; the act of faith is necessarily our own. And yet it cannot be so completely our own that it does not grow out of, and partially reaffirm, the faith of the community.

According to Thomas Aquinas, the authority of the teaching church is merely pedagogic; it is a preliminary that brings us into a situation in which we can personally see what we ought to believe:

There are three things which lead us to the faith of Christ: natural reason, the testimony of the Law and the Prophets, the preaching of the Apostles and others. But when a man has thus been led as it were by the hand to the Faith, then he can say that he believes for none of the preceding motives; not because of natural reason, nor because of the witness of the Law, nor because of the preaching of men, but only because of the Truth itself. . . . It is from the light that God infuses that faith derives its certitude.[8]

In more modern terminology we might say that faith really comes into its own when we no longer believe precisely because of the apologetical arguments which extrinsically point to Christ and the church as organs of revelation, nor because the Bible or the church tells us that we ought to believe as we do, but because we personally derive effective guidance and illumination from what Christianity teaches. Throughout all our religious lives we have to keep striving to appropriate the Christian tradition—to make it real and effective for ourselves—and as we do so we shall find that we are able to express it in new formulas that are authentically our own. In Tillichian terminology we might say that the authority of revelation ceases to be "heteronomous" and becomes "theonomous." [9]

Thus our discussion of the learning process has ineluctably led into our second question—that of personal discovery. By "discovery" I here mean a mental illumination that makes things fall into place. Discovery brings with it a certain firmness of conviction, sometimes so overpowering that we feel it to be irreversible. If personal faith involves discovery, we should ask ourselves at this point what is the place of reason in discovery.

It is sometimes said that reasoning is useless in this sphere. "The great discoverers of principles," writes Newman, "do not reason. . . . It is the second-rate men, though most useful in their place, who prove, reconcile, finish, explain." [10] In his effort to construct what he called a "grammar of assent," Newman piled up instance after instance of the "surplusage of belief over proof." [11] While verbal argument is sometimes useful for outlining the main steps of an inference after it has been made, language is too crude an instrument for the initial discovery, which Newman attributes to a faculty he calls the illative sense. This sense, as Newman explains it, is a spontaneous power of inference, not dependent upon formal rules. In a sentence which some linguistic analysts of our century would do well to ponder, he wrote: "The mind itself is more versatile and vigorous than any of its works, of which language is one, and it is only under its penetrating and subtle action that the margin disappears, which I have described as intervening between verbal argumentation and conclusions in the concrete. It determines what science cannot determine, the limit of converging probabilities and the reasons sufficient for proof." [12]

In an important article on "Faith and Reason," [13] Michael Polanyi proposes as the best paradigm for religious discovery the kind of informal inference that is at work when we recognize comprehensive entities in the objects of our experience. When we come to see a person as a person, rather than as a mere blob of color, we actively synthesize a multitude of details that cannot be exhaustively enumerated. A similar mysterious process is at work when we get meanings out of the words on a printed page, or when a doctor makes a diagnosis. There is no way of specifying in the abstract when there are enough symptoms to warrant a judgment that a victim has epilepsy. Only the skilled physician can say, by applying his acquired prudence to a particular concrete case.

Theologians in the past have generally paid far too little heed to the individual logic of discovery, as outlined by authors such as Newman and Polanyi. It is my conviction that greater attention to this aspect of epistemology could be of immense importance for many questions in apologetics, such as the nature of salvation history, the value of miracles and prophecy, the value of the life of Christ or the saints as signs of faith, the church as a sign of credibility, and the like. In all of these cases we have to do with patterns of intelligibility that point to a divinely given meaning. There is no way of strictly proving that the meaning is really there. Either one recognizes it or one does not. As we contemplate the scene there seem to be moments when the pieces fall into a pattern. It is as though the meaning were given to us; we perceive it as a gift, a grace. And yet we cannot say that reason is not at work. The illative sense reasons in its own way.

The process of religious discovery resembles the recognition of a familiar face, the judgment that someone is making a sign to me, or the diagnosis of a disease. The main difference between these illustrations and the case of religious conviction is that a religious inquirer is concerned with the ultimate meaning of the whole universe, including his own personal existence. To determine the presence of such a meaning one has to rely on clues which permit the divine ground, so to speak, to shine through certain specific events. In a moment of grace we apprehend the infinite, the absolute, the incomprehensible.

If religious meaning, in the moment of recognition, bursts upon one unpredictably, it would seem to follow that faith would not be prerequired in the search. But the contrary must be said. According to Polanyi, the way to find a hidden meaning, even in nonreligious areas of knowledge, is to focus not on the details but on the meaning itself which, although as yet concealed, is believed to be present. In major scientific discoveries, he contends, the investigator is always sustained by a confidence that what he is looking for is really there to be found. "Our heuristic cravings," writes Polanyi, "imply the existence of answers, and only by concentrating on the anticipated solution can we successfully line up the data." [14] When the solution does come, it commands assent because accredited in advance by our confidence that it would be there. Thus the process of discovery turns out to be simply another instance of the general rule, "Unless you believe you shall not understand."

Polanyi's epistemology seems to me to cast light on the perennial question whether we admit the proofs of the existence of God because we already believe in him, or whether we believe because we first learn by reason that God exists. A similar dispute revolves around the question whether we recognize the Christian miracles because we believe in Christianity or accept Christianity because of the miracles. If we look at the proofs of God's existence as

logical syllogisms which would be intended to carry us
from the finite to a completely unknown infinite, the
demonstrations break down. If we look at miracles with
cold detachment, without any personal concern for their
religious meaning, they are opaque to the divine. We must
have in advance some intimation of that which is to emerge
from the signs.

As Augustine and theologians influenced by him have
often said, we would not even be able to look for God
unless we had a prior confidence that our craving for him
had a real object. Before we begin to ask the question
of God we already know him implicitly in the restlessness
of our own hearts, in which he is at work. The active fore-
knowledge of the meaning which is still to emerge in full
clarity is a kind of inchoate faith, and is required to give
reason the necessary direction in its quest. When we do
find in Christ the appearance of God our Savior, we feel
that we are recognizing ("re-cognizing") something we
already knew in an obscure way.

As Polanyi observes, the heuristic process, even in the
physical and mathematical sciences, is sustained by passion.
Hence the discovery, when it occurs, evokes the kind of
heuristic delight expressed prototypically in the "heureka"
of Archimedes.

The great theologians have always been conscious of
the role played by the affections in religious inquiry. The
older Scholastics, including St. Thomas, used to speak in
this connection of a knowledge by connaturality or sympathy.[15] The more a man is akin to God by love or desire,
the more sensitive will he be to the signs of God's presence.
What is a sign to one person may not be a sign to another,
because active receptivity is necessary to enable one to
read the meaning of personal signs. To the lover the
smallest gestures of the beloved are charged with significance which strangers cannot discern. Hence the need for

moral purification and purity of heart for a "real assent" to the divine.

To ask whether reason can demonstrate the existence of God or the credibility of the Christian religion is therefore to put an ambiguous question, to which no simple answer can be given. If the words "reason" and "demonstration" are used in the sense of rigorous deduction from principles self-evident to every man, the answer must be "no." For the proofs to impart true conviction there must be an antecedent openness and concern which can, in some wide sense of the word, be called "faith." The explicit act of faith is a further determination of a primordial or implicit faith, which guides the process of inquiry and serves as a heuristic basis for the interpretation of the signs.

If my contentions in this paper are valid, it must be concluded that in the realm of religious knowledge, and indeed in all knowledge, reason necessarily works on the basis of what may in some wide sense be called "faith." The faith in question—faith antecedent to reason—may be taken on two levels, never adequately distinct. In the first place there is a personal orientation born of an implicit supposition that there is a total meaningfulness to life and the universe. This anticipation of a transcendent or religious meaning directs one's personal process of inquiry and enables one, at times, to discern the divine, thanks to the signs that have been given.

On the second level, that of "authority," faith means a trusting acceptance of the tradition of the community to which one adheres. This confidence may be either weakened or confirmed by personal reflection. If one finds tradition to be a useful guide in making sense of what is known from other sources, one becomes increasingly committed to it. But in reaffirming the tradition we always develop and modify it. Tradition cannot be simply a static collection of answers handed down from the past.

Reason in this framework means the process of verifying whether the anticipations set up by faith are or are not an adequate guide for the interpretation of other data. Reason may lead away from faith but it may also strengthen and develop it. The movement of reason can, and often does, bring faith from an implicit and provisional stage to one that is explicit, personally ratified, and mature.

When faith becomes luminous and leads to understanding, does it cease to be faith? Is the authority that led to faith now cast aside in favor of personal apprehension? This is the common view of rationalists, but it is not, I think, a valid position. The mainstream of Christian thought has consistently opposed such rationalizing tendencies. The encounter with transcendence that constitutes the basis of religious conviction never occurs without the mediation of some created agency—the humanity of Christ, the church, the Scriptures, the sacraments, or whatever. Thus even when one appropriates the Christian faith with the fullness of personal conviction, one remains dependent on external signs to present and commend the content of faith. An element of authority remains.

The authority can be significantly appropriated and internalized, so that one could not relinquish it without forsaking something of one's own, but still it remains to some extent other than oneself. Although pure "theonomy," as Tillich describes it, is always an ideal to which we tend, it is never perfectly realized under the conditions of this life. A measure of "heteronomy" remains. Thus, while insisting that the religious authorities ought not to be viewed in sheerly extrinsicist terms, we acknowledge that man's situation in this life must always remain that of one seeking the fullness of understanding. No matter how advanced he may be, the Christian may rightly be admonished: "Unless you believe, you shall not understand."

Faith and understanding, therefore, enter into a dialectical unity. Understanding and believing are not identical, but it is when I believe that I best understand, and it is when I understand that I believe most fully as I should. The Christian is convinced that the beliefs of his own tradition are capable of leading to the fullest and highest understanding available to man.

NOTES

1. Étienne Gilson, *Reason and Revelation in the Middle Ages* (Charles Scribner's Sons, 1938).

2. H. Richard Niebuhr, *Christ and Culture* (Harper Torchbook, 1956).

3. Blaise Pascal, "Préface sur le traité du vide," *Opuscules et Lettres (Choix)*, ed. by L. Lafuma (Paris: Aubier, 1955), p. 50. My translation.

4. Charles Davis, *A Question of Conscience* (Harper & Row, Publishers, Inc., 1967), pp. 6–8.

5. This formula, taken from the Septuagint translation of Isa. 7:9, is often cited by Augustine: e.g., *De libero arbitrio* 2:2:6 (*PL* 33:1243); *Epist.* 120, c. 1, n. 3 (*PL* 33: 453).

6. Bernard J. Lonergan, "Theology in Its New Context," in L. K. Shook (ed.), *Theology of Renewal,* Vol. 1 (Herder and Herder, 1968), pp. 37–38.

7. Michael Polanyi, *Personal Knowledge: Towards a Post-Critical Philosophy* (Harper Torchbook, 1964), p. 207.

8. Thomas Aquinas, *Comment. in Joann.* IV, lect. 5, a. 2. Cf. the reflections of Jacques Maritain, *The Range of Reason* (Charles Scribner's Sons, 1952), p. 209.

9. Paul Tillich discusses the dialectic of autonomy, heteronomy, and theonomy in many places. See especially his *Systematic Theology* (The University of Chicago Press, 1951), Vol. I, pp. 83–86, 147–150.

10. John H. Newman, *A Grammar of Assent* (London:

Longmans, Green & Company, Ltd. [new impression], 1913),
p. 380.
11. *Ibid.*, p. 300.
12. *Ibid.*, p. 360.
13. Michael Polanyi, "Faith and Reason," *Journal of Religion,* Vol. 41 (1961), pp. 237–247.
14. Polanyi, *op. cit.,* p. 127.
15.   Cf. Thomas Aquinas, *Summa theol.* 2–2, q. 1, a. 4, ad 3;
q. 45, a. 2, c.

III

OFFICIAL CHURCH TEACHING AND HISTORICAL RELATIVITY

Avery Dulles, S.J.

ESPECIALLY perhaps within Roman Catholicism, a doctrinal crisis is going on. Nothing has been more characteristic of Catholicism in the past than a high degree of certainty about a multitude of doctrines. Gradually over the centuries the zone of certitude increased, as more and more doctrines became officially endorsed, even defined, by the magisterium. In the past few centuries it began to appear as though the positions of St. Thomas on most points were destined to become the positions of the church for the rest of time. With its high degree of systematization and its tenacity in adhering to the patristic and medieval tradition, Catholicism became par excellence the church of historical continuity and of organic development. It claimed to offer its members a complete and reliable map of life, together with all the desired aids to navigation.

In the past decade, especially since the end of Vatican II, the uniformity in Catholicism has shown signs of breaking up. It is as though the neatly woven fabric were becoming unraveled. More and more of the accepted doctrines have begun to be questioned or even contested within the church. Some begin by asking, Do we still have to believe in angels? Then they question the Immaculate Conception and the Assumption, then transubstantiation, then the virginal conception of Christ, then papal infallibility, and so on—until the anxious faithful begin to ask, as many do today, What doctrine is exempt from questioning within the church? What can we believe with full and unhesitating conviction?

What is happening? Is it that a spirit of unbelief has been let loose in the church? Are the skepticism and incredulity of the modern world seeping into the church and eroding the structures of faith? If so, we should discountenance these new developments, adhere staunchly to the ancient heritage, and remain loyally by the side of Christ even though the majority of his disciples should desert him.

It would be a mistake, however, to make a facile identification of the present questioning with unbelief. Some of the most radical probing is being done by men who are deeply committed to Christ and to the church. They feel that in criticizing ancient formulations of faith, and in rejecting what seems to be inadequate or false, they are performing a loyal service to the church. They even claim authorization from John XXIII and from Vatican II. Hence the present conflict is not so much between belief and unbelief as between different shades of opinion within the church. Some tend to be conservative and traditional, others liberal and progressive, in the manner in which they formulate their faith.

Terms such as "conservative" and "liberal," of course, are only relative. Every Christian is somewhat conservative, for Christianity means understanding one's life in terms of a past event—the event of Jesus Christ which forms the central theme of the New Testament. If this event were denied or ignored, a man would have no reason to call himself a Christian. On the other hand, no Christian can be completely conservative, for what he understands in the light of Christ must be precisely his own life and his own world. This is something that did not exist for the Biblical authors. The contemporary believer must ask new questions which had not arisen, as such, in Biblical times; and new questions demand answers which are in some respects new.

The problem of the old and the new arises out of the historicity of man. Man is a being who lives out of a remembered past, in a transitory present, toward an anticipated future. To what extent must Christian faith, then, retain the forms which it had in the past? To what extent is it legitimate and necessary to construct new formulas of faith that correspond to our experience and hope today?

Some Catholics would appeal at this point to the distinction between fallible and infallible teaching. They would say that we are free to form new opinions on all those points which have not been settled by unanimous consent of the fathers or by a solemn definition of a pope or general council. Since there are relatively few irreformable pronouncements, this approach seems to provide a large measure of maneuverability.

But this distinction between infallible dogmas and the rest of church teaching is not as helpful for our purposes as one might think. In the first place, there is no agreed list of irreformable decrees, and therefore the distinction does not really tell us what may, and what may not, be questioned. Secondly, the interpretation of admittedly dogmatic statements is not always clear, and thus what one person regards as the very core of the definition will seem to another to be an excessively narrow interpretation of it. Thirdly, many dogmas are as great a stumbling block to the contemporary believer as the nondogmatic statements. Several of the disputed points I mentioned earlier (Immaculate Conception, transubstantiation, infallibility, etc.) have to do with dogmas. If it is not permitted to ask questions about these matters, the "liberals" have lost their case without a hearing. On the other hand, there are so few statements of unquestionably dogmatic status, that to say that they alone constitute the binding content of faith would excessively narrow down the import of Christianity. Thus I do not think that the distinction between fallible and infallible teaching is the true key to our problem.

As a more fruitful approach, I suggest that we focus our attention on the historical relativity of all doctrinal statements. If we recall that the truth of revelation is never known in its naked absoluteness, but is always grasped within the perspectives of a sociocultural situation, we shall have a useful tool for finding out what may be conserved in an unquestionably antiquated formulation, and what ought to be revised in an indubitably authentic expression of the faith. The fact that men in the past expressed the Christian revelation in a manner suited to their own times does not mean that we should reject what they said; nor does it mean that we ought to speak the same way. Our task is to "appropriate" what they said— to make it our own—and to express it in a contemporary form.

This program of modernization is, however, too obvious to be instructive and too vague to be practical. It merely raises the question how we are to distinguish between what some would call the "form" and "content" of an ancient doctrinal statement. Are there any criteria by which we can separate the good grain of revelation from the chaff of historical relativity? Unless such criteria can be found, we shall not get beyond the present impasse, in which the very thing that one theologian regards as a time-conditioned interpretation represents, in the eyes of another, the very substance of the faith.

In these few pages, I have no intention of discussing the

total problem of religious truth and its expression. I shall have to presuppose certain positions that cannot be defended here. I assume, for instance, that revelation is salvific truth; it necessarily has to do with the redemption of mankind and of the world. Merely historical or scientific information, considered in itself, cannot possibly be the true content of revelation. Furthermore, I take for granted that the salvific truth is, most centrally, the mystery of God's vital self-communication, which comes to us as a call to transcend our limited self-interest and to entrust ourselves to God. This mystery of the divine self-communication cannot be spoken of with the same clarity and objectivity that can be sought in discussing things familiar to us from our ordinary experience. I presuppose, moreover, that when a man speaks about the themes of revelation, he necessarily has to use concepts and terms drawn from his experience in the world. We cannot designate the saving mysteries except with the help of ideas and terminology supplied by the culture in which we live. In Scripture, in Christian tradition, and in the contemporary church the word of God comes to us in and through the culturally conditioned words of men. Finally, I shall assume that church teaching over the centuries has been, by and large, an accurate, though not always a fully balanced, articulation of the Christian faith.

As regards the binding force of church teaching, there are several pertinent principles that have no particular connection with the problem of historical relativity, but which should be kept in mind in connection with all that follows. In the first place, as already mentioned, not all church documents have the same degree of authority. The extempore remarks of the pope at an audience in the Vatican may represent simply his personal feelings at the moment, and need not be always taken as official teaching. Even when a pope or bishop intends to make use of his power as an authoritative teacher, it is not to be presumed that the utterances are infallible definitions. Only very rarely does the magisterium invoke its defining power.[1]

Secondly, it should be clear that in any magisterial statement, however authoritative, a distinction must be made between the point of the affirmation and the supporting statements. There is nothing new or unusual about this principle. Lawyers, for example, often distinguish between the decision of the court, which constitutes a normative precedent, and the reasoning of the court, which is as valid as the arguments proposed. *Obiter dicta* are in no way binding. Scripture scholars have ably distinguished between the degrees of affirmation in the Bible. "Here is the definite affirmation, there is also the statement of a probability, or of a possibility, even of a mere conjecture or of a doubt." [2] So, too, in documents of the church, any skilled theologian must know how to distinguish between what the church was intending to teach, and the statements introduced merely for the sake of clarification, persuasion, or edification. The standard manuals of theology, in their treatment of the "notes" or "censures," give some helpful rules of thumb, but it cannot be said that this problem has generally received the attention it deserves.[3]

As regards the interpretation of authoritative statements, the true point of the affirmation is often best discerned by studying the historical context. One must know why the magisterium was speaking, what error it was rejecting. As Schoonenberg remarks, "If a pronouncement is issued against a certain opinion, its positive statements should be interpreted in the first place as a defence against the condemned opinion and not as the only possible definition of the mystery which is being defended." [4] Generally speaking, this principle is an excellent guide, though it may happen that the positive statement is the only conceivable alternative to the condemned opinion—as the divinity of the Christ is the only possible alternative to the condemned proposition that the Son is a creature.

With these preambles in mind, let us now turn to the specific question that presently concerns us: how to distinguish between the truth of revelation and its time-bound formulations. The following six principles are, I believe, important.

1. In the interpretation of doctrinal statements, heed should be paid to variations in literary conventions.

This principle, obvious though it may sound, has frequently been violated in traditional theology. For centuries efforts were made to force the Bible into the framework of Greek and Western literary forms, and to treat apparently scientific and historical statements in Scripture as though they had to conform to what a modern European might mean if he made the same statements. In Catholic teaching, an immense step forward was made when the encyclical *Divino Afflante Spiritu* (1943) officially acknowledged that the authors of the Bible employed the forms and modes of speech in use among the people of their own place and time, and that therefore the exegete, instead of deciding a priori what forms ought to have been used, should base his decision on the evidence of what the Biblical authors actually did do.[5] Largely as a result of this encyclical, confirmed by the teaching of Vatican II,[6] Catholic exegesis today has no hesitation in recognizing in the Bible metaphor, hyperbole, pseudonymity, and the conventional use of prophetic and apocalyptic imagery.

This principle of literary forms has important implications for theology. The Biblical scholar today feels free to admit discrepancies which would formerly have been regarded as scientific and historical errors. Further, he does not feel obliged to take literally many statements which were previously thought to refer to miraculous divine interventions. For example, the fact that a Biblical book begins, "The word of the Lord came to the prophet x, saying . . ." does not necessarily imply that the words that follow are the direct discourse of Yahweh himself.

What has not yet been done, in sufficient detail, is to subject official church documents to form-critical analysis. We too often forget that popes and councils sought to speak in ways common for high officials of their time, and that they were aiming not simply to communicate a content but to do so in a manner that would evoke a suitable emotional and practical response on the part of the faithful. Ecclesiastical pronouncements from the Middle Ages until the First Vatican Council (inclusively) commonly were phrased in a majestic, even triumphalistic, style that would not be considered appropriate today. In order to arouse feelings of awe and confidence, the church presented her doctrine as "most certain," "most evident," and branded the contrary views as blasphemous and absurd. Erring Christians were accused of being proud, stubborn, and shameless in their adulteration of the word of God, and were threatened with eternal penalties if they failed to submit. Vatican II, speaking to a twentieth-century audience, avoided the pyrotechnics of dogmatic definition and anathematization. When we go back to earlier church documents, we should not read them as if they were written yesterday. We must be on guard against mistaking merely rhetorical superlatives for substantive teaching. If hyperbole is to be admitted in the Bible, who is to deny that it may also be found in ecclesiastical pronouncements?

2. An antiquated world view, presupposed but not formally taught in an earlier doctrinal formulation, should not be imposed as binding doctrine.

As far as the Bible is concerned, this principle was the heart of Rudolf Bultmann's demythologizing program. In his famous essay on "New Testament and Mythology" [7] he argued that the New Testament, in its presentation of the events of redemption, presupposes an essentially mythical view of the world as a three-storied structure, with the earth at the center, the heavens above, and the underworld beneath. In such a world view, he says, it was taken for granted that the earth was the scene of the supernatural activity of God and his angels, and of Satan and his demons. Possession and miracles were deemed to be common occurrences. The New Testament writers did not invent this world view; they did not teach it; they simply took it for granted as something accepted by the milieu in which they lived. They presented the gospel in terms of the accepted ideas of their time.

In order to preach the gospel today, it would be pointless to try to force twentieth-century men to accept a first-century cosmology. We ought to be able to present the Biblical message in terms of a modern world view. Otherwise we would be illegitimately adding to the content of the gospel by requiring people to accept a strange and incredible world view which was not part of the original gospel, but was simply an unquestioned presupposition at the time the New Testament was written.

To some extent Christians always have modified the Biblical world view in accordance with the accepted ideas of their own time. The medieval theologians, nurtured on Greek philosophy, took it for granted that God must be pure spirit, immutable, impassible, etc. When they found statements in the Bible about God changing, or becoming angry, or repenting what he had done, they took these to be metaphors. A writer such as St. Thomas conceives of God and of God's relationship to the world in a way quite foreign to Biblical thought, but we have become so habituated to the Thomistic conception that it no longer strikes us as a daring innovation. Today the cosmology of St. Thomas is almost as antiquated as that of the Bible, and it is necessary to restate the Christian message in terms of a contemporary world view. Teilhard de Chardin made one attempt to do so, and we may expect that there will be others. As these efforts are made, many classical theological conceptions will no doubt be transformed. It is hard to predict what may happen to the currently accepted ideas of creation, inspiration, miracle, resurrection, etc. We must be prepared for revisions insofar as the traditional notions are to some extent bound up with an obsolete cosmology.

3. Technical terms should be interpreted in terms of the systematic framework presupposed by those who used them.

A great deal of Christian doctrine in the patristic era and in the Middle Ages is based on conceptual structures taken over from Greek philosophy. While Christian theology refined the categories of Greek philosophy, it did not essentially change them. It continued to presuppose the dichotomies of time and eternity, spirit and matter, substance and accident which had prevailed in Platonic and Aristotelian philosophy. If a theologian today were to accept a radically different philosophical system, such as one finds in modern personalistic phenomenology or process philosophy, he would have to transpose many of the Christian doctrines in a manner that might sound like a rejection. But to try to introduce these doctrines unchanged into a new philosophical framework would be impossible, or would amount to an ever greater deformation.

As a case in point, one might cite the recent dispute about the term "transubstantiation." In terms of a commonsense substance philosophy, it is meaningful to say that Christ takes the place of the "whole substance" of the bread. But if one denies that there ever was such a thing as the "substance of the bread" or that physical realities are made up of substance and accident, it becomes almost necessary to speak of the "real presence" in a new way. To find satisfactory equivalents in other philosophical systems is a task of creative theology.

4. In the interpretation of Biblical and theological terms, cognizance should be taken of connotation as well as denotation.

The terminology of the Bible is concrete, imaginative, and conceptually imprecise. A great deal has been lost when theologians have tried to pick out terms from the Bible and give them exact, abstract definitions. When we read in the New Testament, for instance, that we have been redeemed by the blood of Christ (Rom. 3:25; Heb. 9:13–14; 13:12; I Peter 1:19), we are not dealing with terms that admit of any simple definition. They are laden with connotations from the exodus, the temple worship, and the Mosaic Law. In general it may be said that redemption by the blood of Jesus did not mean to the New Testament authors what it spontaneously suggests to the modern Western mind. Especially since Anselm, the terms "redemption" and "blood" have taken on new significances and have largely lost the significance they had to the ancient Semite. The notion of making reparation to the offended honor of God by offering up the blood of an innocent victim is more medieval than Biblical.

Today, when the Biblical conception of redemption has become almost unintelligible and the Anselmian doctrine repugnant, there is urgent need for forging a new vocabulary of redemption. One might well begin by so immersing himself in the Biblical tradition as to grasp what the New Testament authors meant by their soteriological terms. In order to find suitable equivalents, one would probably have to come at the whole problem of sin, salvation, and new life in God from a new direction. The Biblical and medieval terms are so imbedded in the context of patriarchal and feudal forms of life that they have become almost unserviceable for popular usage.

5. No doctrinal decision of the past directly solves a question that was not asked at the time.

Biblical and conciliar texts have often been abused to make them answer questions that are asked today but were not in the minds of the original authors. For example, Paul in Romans and the Council of Trent, quoting Paul, assert that Adam was a single man, and that he is the source of original sin. Modern science has raised the question whether the human race might not be descended from more than one original couple. Some theologians have invoked the authority of Paul and Trent to refute polygenism. But to this it may legitimately be objected that neither of these texts was dealing formally with the question of the origins of the human race, and further that the question of monogenism vs. polygenism had not even arisen at the time. They spoke in passing of Adam as a single individual because this seemed to them to be the obvious interpretation of Genesis, but it may be doubted whether they wished to settle authoritatively a question which could scarcely have entered their minds.[8] For us today, the matter is not so simple. For one thing, the teaching of Genesis on the point is far from clear. In some passages the term "Adam" must be interpreted as a collective noun, signifying mankind (both male and female). More importantly, the man of today would scarcely go to the Creation narrative in Genesis to solve a scientific question such as the origins of man. If Paul and the fathers at Trent did so, it was because the historicity of Genesis was something they took for granted. Precisely because they took it for granted, they were never forced to reflect on the matter, and hence they could not have settled any subsequent disputes which might arise about the historicity of the early chapters in Genesis.

This general principle—that nobody can decisively answer a question that has not come up at the time[9]—has very wide application in dogmatic theology. For example, Christian tradition for at least fifteen hundred years was virtually unanimous in accepting the physical universality of the Flood. Yet we cannot draw up a valid proof from a morally unanimous consensus on the question. A significant consensus would have to follow from a reflective weighing of the pros and cons such as could scarcely have taken place until more information had been gathered about the literary forms of Genesis and the data of paleontology. Today almost nobody imagines that the universality of the Flood can be proved from the naïve statements of Scripture or church tradition.

A more difficult question occurs where the magisterium attempts to settle a question and it later turns out that the decision was based on inadequate information. This occurred many times with decisions of the Biblical Commission in the first two decades of the twentieth century. Anxious to head off new ideas that might undermine the faith of Catholics, the Biblical Commission took very conservative positions, which later proved impossible to defend. In 1955 officials of the Commission acknowledged that previous decrees on critical or historical questions, insofar as these were based on the state of the evidence at the time, were subject to revision.[10]

Extending this principle we can perhaps say that whenever the state of the evidence on any question materially changes, you have a new question, which cannot be fully answered by appealing to old authorities.[11] If this were admitted, some very interesting discussions could arise with regard to decisions made at Trent and even Vatican I. Some of the Scriptural and historical arguments on which the fathers relied would not stand up very well in view of what is known today about the formation of the New

Testament. Perhaps new arguments can be fashioned that prove the same conclusions; but perhaps also the conclusions might be said to admit of some modification since they were not, and could not have been, based on evidence that would today be convincing. To give but one example, I doubt whether any well-informed theologian, if he were speaking for the first time on the subject, would think of saying, as did Vatican I, that Christ made Peter "prince of all the apostles and visible head of the entire Church militant," and gave him "primacy of true and proper jurisdiction." [12] The phraseology, at least, is bound up with the political experience of Western Europe in a certain historical era. If the question were coming up for new decision today, we would doubtless look for other ways of talking about the Petrine office in conformity with current New Testament scholarship and contemporary political forms.

6. In Holy Scripture and in authoritative doctrinal statements, one should be alert for signs of social pathology and ideology.

The church, since New Testament times (inclusively), has been an organization of weak and sinful men. At no time in history have Christians been free from fear, anxiety, resentment. Those in authority are naturally inclined to govern in a way that increases the docility of the faithful, even if this means suppressing certain facts that might raise embarrassing questions. Often the faithful themselves like to attribute magical powers to their leaders, partly in order to stimulate their corporate pride in the organization, and partly to relieve themselves of responsibility for their own religious positions. These ideological factors go far to explain the peculiarities of curial rhetoric on which I have already commented. Charles Davis, after expressing the desire that a literary expert should study ecclesiastical language, remarks quite correctly: "Hyperbole in support of the established order and accepted doctrines or in fear-provoking condemnation of vaguely adumbrated errors is greatly encouraged." [13] "Above all, there is never an admission of past error or a frank avowal that present statements contradict past teaching." [14]

Gregory Baum, in his reply to Davis,[15] points out that what Davis is criticizing is a type of social pathology to which the church as a religious institution is particularly subject. He shows how in the New Testament community itself sociopathological forces were at work, causing the early Christians to project their inadequacies and failures upon the Jews who had not accepted Christianity. Much of the defensiveness and fanaticism in the church, especially in the post-Tridentine period, can be sociologically explained. When the traditional claims of the church were contested by the Protestants, Catholics reacted by insisting exorbitantly on the divine powers and infallibility of the church. Only in Vatican II do we see a change for the better. Here the church frankly recognizes that she, as an institution, is affected by sin, and must constantly pursue the path of repentance and reform. In *Gaudium et Spes* the Council admits that the church has no answer to many of the troublesome questions of our time, and that she must humbly listen to what competent specialists have to say.[16]

For anyone reading the older church documents, it is important to make allowance for sociological factors that may have led to narrowness (some interpretations of the axiom, *extra Ecclesiam nulla salus!*), exorbitant claims (the bull, *Unam Sanctam!*), harshness toward adversaries, and the like. The divine truth is not taught by the church in divine form, but in a human form, and thus it is always difficult to draw the line between what is of faith and what is to be set aside as a human perversion. The more precious the truth, and the more esteemed it is in the community, the more the heirs of the tradition are tempted to indulge in pride, fanaticism, and calumny.

At the beginning of this paper I called attention to the doctrinal crisis in the church today. The question arose, Why are so many doctrines, which were apparently in peaceful possession for many centuries, suddenly being questioned from within the church? If my argument has been sound, we are now in a position to give a partial answer. After a long period of resistance, historical relativity has broken through into Catholic theology. Any sophisticated theologian today knows that he has to reckon with the historical conditioning of all ecclesiastical statements. Every pronouncement has to be critically analyzed in terms of sociocultural factors. What was the historical *Sitz im Leben* out of which it arose? What literary conventions and figures of speech were employed in its formulation? What general picture of the world was simply taken for granted by the authors? What philosophical categories did they presuppose as the framework for their concepts? What was the full connotation of the terms to the men who first used them to express the mysteries of revelation? What precise question was in the minds of the authors, and how does it differ from the question that confronts us today? What effects of human weakness and sinfulness can be noted in the formulation of the doctrine itself?

Some may feel that the emphasis of this paper has been excessively negative, but my intention is to clear the way for a more positive appreciation of the tradition. Many people reject ecclesiastical authority because they think it prevents them from criticizing the defects of past presentations of the Christian message. In my opinion it is only when we have been able to recognize and, so to speak, "siphon off" the human limitations and distortions that we are able to discover in and behind the faulty words of men the divine truth that is coming to expression through, and partly in spite of, its human witnesses. Once revelation is rightly understood as a divine action, it is obvious that there can be no absolute equation between the word of God and the words of men. But there can be a paradoxical or dialectical identity between the two. Consciousness of the historical relativity of all human utterances, far from negating the word of God, enables us to situate the human coefficient, and thus to perceive more clearly the truth that is divine.

To acknowledge the relativity of historical formulations, then, is not to fall prey to relativism, but rather to escape imprisonment within the historical limitations of any one cultural period.[17] The present helps us to liberate ourselves from the tyranny of the past, and the past, to escape the idolatry of the present. The truth of revelation, in a mysterious way, preserves its dynamic identity amid the changing formulations. Each of the formulations must justify itself as an authentic articulation of the one gospel to which Christians are committed in faith. The truth of the gospel must come to us through human formulas, for otherwise it could not reach us where we are. It does not come to us in any eternally valid representations, because man's concepts are necessarily drawn from the fluctuating world in which he finds himself.

As we face the task of restating the Christian message for the twentieth century, we must of course beware of prematurely jettisoning formulas that are still meaningful, and that serve to link us with the past. It would be a tragedy if the current confessional formulas failed to manifest the unity of our faith with that of the apostles, and if they no longer pointed back to the experience of the first Christians. We certainly do not want a diluted version of the gospel—one that would sacrifice anything of the revelation given, once and for all, in Christ. Christianity must always retain its solid anchorage in the unrepeatable events of the first century.

It is important likewise for the church to maintain a vital link with the earlier stages of its own tradition. If all doctrinal formulations are inadequate, it stands to reason that traditional statements, no longer in the current idiom, may often have something to offer as correctives to more current expressions. History, after all, is not all progress. Biblical anthropology, had it been taken more seriously in the seventeenth century, would have offered a healthy corrective to Cartesian dualism. So, too, in our time, we should not be too hasty in writing off the positive value of a medieval doctrine such as "transubstantiation." Even if the formula is unassimilable into modern metaphysics, it remains valid as a testimony to the ancient faith of the church. Even doctrinal statements that are inconsistent with our world view may be susceptible of a "retrieve" (in the Heideggerian sense), and thus deserve to be retained in dynamic tension with more recent conceptualizations.[18]

To prevent the gospel from losing its impact, however, we must not shirk the task of modernization. It is not enough to repeat the verbal formulations of an earlier time, or even to translate them, one by one, into a new idiom. We live in an age that differs radically from anything that went before. Mankind has been projected, as it were, overnight into the electronic age. As a result, the Christian message as a whole must be refocused in a way that speaks immediately and directly to the deepest concerns of the present. Such a creative refocusing cannot be achieved by simply finding new equivalents for old terms and formulas. Vatican II recognized that dogmas are not isolated statements, but are articulations of a single vision, some closer to, and some more distant from, the heart of the Christian mystery.[19] In restating the Christian message for our day we need a system of dogmas that develops organically out of what our faith has to say most urgently to contemporary man. Some dogmas that were very functional and important for systems based on a different perspective will perhaps have less prominence, although they will not be directly contradicted, in new, dynamic restatements of the faith.

If new questions demand new answers, the function of tradition cannot be simply to transmit materially what has been said in the past, but rather to provide effective guidelines for achieving Christian answers to current questions. It is not enough to repeat what our predecessors have said; we must imitate their courage and leadership. There is no reason why the church today should not offer men a richer fare of truth, inspiration, and guidance than ever before. Our contemporaries need what the church ought to be able to say. They are no less bewildered, victimized, and dejected than the people of Palestine in the first century. They are still like sheep without a shepherd. We cannot nourish them with the stale fragments of a meal prepared for believers of the fourth or the thirteenth or the sixteenth century. A theology adapted to the times must be based on a fully modern understanding of man and the world. It may be as different from the medieval systems as the computer is from the abacus. Thinkers of the stature of Paul Tillich, Teilhard de Chardin, and Marshall McLuhan have pointed the way. From such a creative theology new doctrinal insights will emerge and they, in turn, may crystallize into new dogmas.

These new dogmas, like their predecessors, will be vital for a time. But eventually, when the perspectives of man's consciousness shift again, they too will lose their actuality. They will serve their purpose if they orient the men of their own time to Christ, who is the same yesterday, today, and forever (Heb. 13:8), and if they help to relay the Christian message to ages yet to come.

NOTES

1. See Vatican II, Constitution on the Church (*Lumen Gentium*), n. 25, in W. M. Abbott, S.J. (ed.), *The Documents of Vatican II* (Guild Press, America Press, Association Press, 1966), pp. 47–50.

2. Pierre Benoit, O.P., "Inspiration," p. 44, in A. Robert and A. Tricot (eds.), *Guide to the Bible* 1 (Desclee Co., Inc. [Division of Herder and Herder], rev. ed., 1960).

3. See, for example, the excursus "De valore et censura propositionum in Theologia," by I. Nicolau, S.J., in *Sacrae Theologiae Summa* 1 (Madrid: B.A.C., 2d ed., 1952), pp. 781–796.

4. P. Schoonenberg, S.J., "Some Remarks on the Present Discussion of Original Sin," *Information Documentation on the Conciliar Church*, No. 68–4 (Jan. 28, 1967), p. 10.

5. *Divino Afflante Spiritu* 35 (1943), pp. 309 ff.; see esp. p. 315; selection in Denzinger-Schönmetzer, *Enchiridion Symbolorum* (Freiburg im Breisgau, 32d ed., 1963), n. 3830.

6. *Dei Verbum*, n. 12; in Abbott (ed.), *op. cit.*, p. 120.

7. Rudolf Bultmann, "New Testament and Mythology," in *Kerygma and Myth*, ed. by H. W. Bartsch (Harper Torchbook, 1961), pp. 1–44.

8. Cf. Karl Rahner, "Evolution and Original Sin," *Concilium*, Vol. 26 (1967), pp. 62–63.

9. Schoonenberg, in the article cited in n. 4 above, lays down as a hermeneutical principle: "A text does not give a direct answer to questions which were not asked at the moment of origin." Then he states the content of this principle in positive form so as to obtain a second principle: "Texts should be interpreted according to their final affirmation according to the question which they seek to answer"; *art. cit.*, pp. 8–9.

10. Cf. E. F. Siegman, "The Decrees of the Pontifical Biblical Commission: A Recent Clarification," *Catholic Biblical Quarterly*, Vol. 18 (1956), pp. 23–29.

11. Thus Hans Küng can write: "The decisions of the Council of Trent (or of other councils) cannot be regarded as binding definitions where they concern questions which are being put differently today in the light of different problems. The Fathers of those days could not decide upon matters they did not know about. This applies particularly to new exegetical and historical problems, which arose only in recent times and need new solutions. No council is granted a fresh revelation; its solutions are tied to the capacities of the theology of its time." (*The Church* [Sheed & Ward, Inc., 1968], p. 419.)

12. Vatican I, *Pastor Aeternus*; in Denzinger-Schönmetzer, *op. cit.*, n. 3055.

13. Charles Davis, *A Question of Conscience* (Harper & Row, Publishers, Inc., 1967), p. 65.

14. *Ibid.*

15. Gregory Baum, *The Credibility of the Church Today* (Herder and Herder, 1968). Baum treats the same point compactly and incisively in his article "The Problem of the Magisterium Today," *Information Documentation on the Conciliar Church*, No. 67–32/33 (Oct. 8, 1967), pp. 13–15.

16. *The Church in the Modern World*, nn. 43–44; in Abbott (ed.), *op. cit.*, pp. 242–246.

17. For an excellent treatment of the problem of reinterpreting dogmatic formulas without falling into relativism, see Edward Schillebeeckx, *God: The Future of Man* (Sheed & Ward, Inc., 1968), Ch. 1, "Towards a Catholic Use of Hermeneutics." Along similar lines see W. Kasper, "Geschichtlichkeit der Dogmen?" in *Stimmen der Zeit*, Vol. 179 (1967), pp. 401–416; George Vass, "On the Historical Structure of Christian Truth," *Heythrop Journal*, Vol. 9 (1968), pp. 129–142, 274–289.

18. Cf. William J. Richardson, *Heidegger: Through Phenomenology to Thought* (The Hague: Nijhoff, 1963), p. 93: "What appears as 'thoughtful dialogue' in the Heidegger of 1950 finds its roots in the existential analysis as re-trieve, by which the Being of There-being becomes explicitly open with regard to the past to such an extent that the full force of Being strikes There-being as if coming out of the future."

19. The Decree on Ecumenism spoke of the order or "hierarchy" in Catholic doctrines, which "vary in their relationship to the foundation of the Christian faith" (n. 11; in Abbott [ed.], *op. cit.,* p. 354).

IV

THE LIMITS OF PLURALISM IN DOCTRINE AND WORSHIP

Carl E. Braaten

INTRODUCTION

After Dietrich Bonhoeffer's brief visit to America in 1939, he wrote an evaluation of American Christianity in an essay entitled "Protestantism Without Reformation." In it he lamented that "it has been granted to the Americans less than any other nation on earth to realize the visible unity of the church of God." [1] Any observer of the religious landscape in America would have to agree. Nowhere and never has there existed so many varieties of Christianity, so many churches, denominations, or synods. America is the land of religious pluralism. In this situation the ecumenical movement has come as a challenge. Our separate churches have been confronted by the ideal of the unity of the church, and they have felt shame for the lack of this attribute. The ecumenical generation spoke enthusiastically of the rediscovery of the church. The churches emerged from behind their walls of hostility into the open forum of dialogue. Many were hoping that as we discussed our differences, we could discover our unity. The drive toward unity would neutralize our diversities. We could find a common denominator. If you take evangelical and episcopal and reformed and catholic traditions, you can merge them by taking something of each, and building them around a common core. That is now being attempted by the Consultation on Church Union (COCU). Methodist, Episcopalian, Presbyterian, Disciples of Christ, and at least a half dozen of other American denominations are going to be merged in one great church body. The Lutherans and the Baptists are the two main holdouts. And, of course, Roman Catholics and Eastern Orthodox are not represented either. Nevertheless, it looks like at least some of the Protestants are doing something about Bonhoeffer's lamentation. They are trying to realize a greater degree of visible unity in the church of Christ. They are in a mood of repentance for their denominationalism, and each is prepared to sacrifice something for the sake of a greater unity.

Since I happen to be a Lutheran, and therefore one of the holdouts, it may appear in poor taste for me to raise the slightest doubt about this church union. But I must confess that I am not enthusiastic, and, even more, I have no strong urge to get the Lutherans into that "bag." It seems to me to be an overly ripe fruit of the ecumenical ethos that is now all but passed. And you know what overly ripe fruit is like: it is soft and mushy, and not very good for eating. This is no place to write a brief in defense of this allegation, but it gives me the occasion to lead into the topic I wish to discuss: the limits of pluralism in doctrine and worship. It seems to me that the models of unity that we constructed in the ecumenical period just passed are unable to cope with pluralism. Our pluralism is a continuing source of embarrassment. It is felt as an obstacle to unity. It is something at best to be tolerated. We have secret regrets that others are not more like us. We may even harbor the hope that after the union we will succeed in winning others over to our way of looking at things. So I have heard some Lutherans argue that they ought to join COCU in order to get others to accept some sound Lutheran doctrine. And in return we might get episcopal succession, presbyterian orderliness, and methodist affectionateness, or whatever it is that Methodists are supposed to have. Well, I don't think that this recipe will make a very good cake, not even if it had the Lutheran ingredient of *sacra pura doctrina*. I do not believe that it is a genuine way to handle the problem of pluralism, and I do not believe that it holds much promise for the future. As with the remarriage of grandmother, one doesn't expect much in the way of offspring.

I am certainly not about to unveil a perfect plan for church union. I have nothing to say to the leaders of COCU. I think they should go ahead with their plan as a way of getting the heirs of Anglo-Saxon Christendom into some positive relations with each other, and thus mainly as a move to compensate for mistakes made in the past. Meanwhile, we cannot see here a model for the larger reunification of the church. At the present time I do not believe that we have a model of unity that could embrace the different histories of Eastern and Western Christianity, of Roman and Reformation Christianity, of the younger churches in the Third World and the mother churches from the colonial nations. But whatever model we develop in the future, it will have to comprehend the phenomenon of pluralism as integral to the church. Pluralism is here to stay; it will be on the increase. The church will need to develop her self-understanding in such a way that pluralism is not regarded as a negative factor, as at best a necessary evil. The modern church will have to do this pretty much from scratch, for in the past the church has been offended by pluralism. Whenever it was necessary for men to break out of a static mold of uniformity, to bring differentiation into a homogenized Christianity, the leaders of the church responded by defining limits more narrowly. Church history is strewn with evidences of the failure to cope with pluralism in the form of the many schisms, sects and heresies, anathemas and excommunications. And often it has happened that the heresy of one day becomes the orthodoxy of the next, that the offense by virtue of which a man is excommunicated one day is sufficient reason to make him a saint another. In struggling to define the boundaries of her true reality, the church has made many mistakes and has sinned against those who bear prophetic witness in behalf of the church's own future.

Now is the time for the church to explore the possibilities of pluralism that her true nature opens up; here in America is a good place to do it. That shocking diversity which Bonhoeffer lamented as a blot against American Christianity may in the longer run turn out to be an asset. For the amazing diversities of Christian expression in America make her a laboratory in which the project of a new pluralistic shape of unity may be worked out in the course of history. We do not have that polymorphous shape already, but in creating a new shape we will no longer express that contempt for pluralism which our monolithic images and uniform structures of the past engendered. I wish to develop an understanding of pluralism as a structural dimension of the church in two steps: (1) the necessity of pluralism in the church as an eschatological community in history; (2) the limits of pluralism in the church as a missionary community in the world, which receives its ongoing identity with reference to its historical origin.

I. THE NECESSITY OF PLURALISM

The starting point for a new appreciation of pluralism can be none other than the church's eschatological character. For the New Testament the church is an eschatological event that takes on historical extension. The church is defined by her relation to the Kingdom of God which Jesus proclaimed in his parables and pioneered in his ministry of love. This Kingdom of God was no little slice of reality; it was not another world after this world, a postponement of payment to religious people who did enough good deeds; nor was it an inner world in the depths of mystical feeling or personal piety. The Kingdom of God was the coming of God's future as the fulfillment of his promises for the world. The church was called into existence from out of the many nations, to be a sacrament of the world's future in the Kingdom of God. The church is to bring to a head what in the world God's Kingdom is struggling to realize; she is to focus the light of God's future on the world. The church is to bear the tidings of good news to the world of its essential future in the fullness of God. Therefore, in being oriented to the Kingdom of God, the church must exist for the world. The concern for the world is not an extracurricular activity. The church should cease thinking of herself as nonworld, as antithetical to the world. For what the church already in a sense enjoys is what the world still has in store for her. There is nothing the church can claim to possess that is not there in principle also for the world. The church exists ahead of the world as the bearer of signs and promises that reach out to encompass the totality of reality on the way to its future destiny.

Now, because the church is defined by her calling to function in behalf of the Kingdom of God for the world, she must be open to new things that happen on the front line of history. That is the source of a pluralism that flourishes in a church that exists in tension between the Kingdom of God and the world. Pluralism is of the essence of a church that functions on the borderlines of the new and the old, of a church that is open in all directions, and not least to the future. The new reality of God's Kingdom places the church in a pioneering role. She explores and she experiments with the forms of the world, to see which of them can be integrated into the multidimensional unity of mankind in the Kingdom of God. The church does not contemn, but affirms the fragmentary and partial anticipations of God's Kingdom that can already be found in the world. The church affirms the many forms of psychological and sociological life; she affirms the various conditions of life that have to do with sex and age and tribe and language and race and culture and nationality. She invites all of them to make ready for, and to take part in, the fulfilled Kingdom of God. Because the church is wide open to the future, she must be wide open to the ways in which the Kingdom is opening up the world to inherit the promises of life and salvation. If the church is to be a microcosm of the world's future, she must bear more of the world's pluriformity than she does now, and in a more cheerful way.

Vast changes are occurring in all churches. Many who have their eye on the values of tradition are worried about all this tinkering with doctrine and tampering with the liturgy. What if what Pope John XXIII intended to be a reformation turns out to be a revolution? Then the changes which now look like tinkering and tampering will be escalated to the desolation and destruction of the church. Fearful of revolution, some want to call a halt to any more changes. Enough is enough! But I think this is a mistaken way of thinking. First of all, experience has proven that the way to avert a revolution is to begin a reform and to carry it out quickly and thoroughly enough. It is always the reactionaries who bear responsibility for revolution, for they hold out against change until the breaking point has been reached. And then it is too late for the reformers. Enter the revolutionaries.

Where are we at in the church today? Is it too late for the reformers? And isn't it a revolution that is needed in the church anyway? Obviously, we will not make any progress using these worn-out labels. We need to see into the matter itself, and to be free from superficial calculations as to whether we have gone far enough or already too far in changing things. We must understand the *telos* of change, the reason for change, and the things that need to be changed. We must win the freedom to change and the courage to change. All these things can be derived from the church's function to use the things of the world in symbolizing the shape and power of God's Kingdom. The church by herself is not equal to this task. The church does not have her own material with which to build. There is no raw material that comes with the label "for church use only." Ecclesiocentrism is the original sin of the church; it leads to the pretension that the church is self-sufficient, that she already has enough stored up in her own sacred traditions on which to live and build for the future. This dispensing with the world throws the church in upon herself, leading to the absolutizing of a sacred sphere, of a sacred style, of a sacred theology, of a sacred language, of sacred forms of art, music, and architecture. Then the cultural forms of the world's antiquity are imagined to be nearer to the Kingdom of God. Here we find echoes of the pagan mythology which says that the farther back you go to the beginning, the closer you get to perfection. The golden age lies in the past. There have always been Christians who have felt that the present is at the point of the greatest distance from the Kingdom, and the less you have to do with your own culture the better.

When the church denies the world and affirms only her past, she is in revolt against the Kingdom and in love with herself. This is at least one source of her failure to cope with pluralism as a positive and necessary dimension of the life of the church. The church's pluralism stems from a relation to the world that is assigned her by the Kingdom of God. We must now try to be more concrete about what this means in present-day terms.

Until a very short time ago practically all churches could expect and even guarantee a broad consensus of doctrine within their ranks. Now every confessional group is penetrated by a multiplicity of beliefs on every basic doctrine. One reason is the ecumenical one: when churches enter into dialogue with each other, they open themselves to a plurality of creedal and doctrinal expressions. Some of these will appear more potent and persuasive than those of their own tradition. But a second reason is the apologetic one: when churches enter into dialogue with the world, they open themselves to an indefinite variety of new styles and new methods, new conditions of experience and knowledge. The church builds new doctrine by taking new cognitive materials from her surrounding culture into her theological life. This is a source of pluralism which the churches cannot control. The churches cannot shut off the water of the world's cultural creativity. Neither can the churches ignore it. In opening themselves to new cultural forms, the churches are driven beyond themselves and beyond the comforting familiarity of their own traditions. Theologians receive impulses to new conceptualization from the various new styles of thought. We can trace the effects of phenomenological, existentialist, linguistic analytic, and dialectical materialist types of philosophy on the recent developments in theology. This is not as such a sign of weakness in theology, that it sways to and fro with every new wind of doctrine. Rather, it can be a symptom of health and vitality when theology seeks to construct its thinking on the basis of the categories of knowledge and criteria of rationality that are generally available to the philosophers.

When we turn from the doctrinal to the liturgical realm, we find a similar necessity for pluralism in a dynamically open community. The church cannot express her spiritual life without using aesthetic forms. There are no cultural forms that are ready-made for religious use. In using forms of art to express her convictions of faith, the church is bearing witness to a structural correspondence between creation and the eschatological future. The Kingdom of God is celebrated already in the use of everyday things of creation. The poetic, musical, and visual forms are "bent" to make manifest the nearness of God's future for those who have experienced his presence in the Christ-happening.

The creative artists of the church have unique demands placed on them.[2] First, they must be sensitive to the range of meanings in the symbols of the Christian tradition. Secondly, they must respect the integrity of the aesthetic media, bending them without violating them. Thirdly, they must dare to use new styles that seem religiously empty and profane alongside the consecrated forms of the tradition. Fourthly, they must have the courage to refuse imitations of what seemed sacred in the past, and to live, as it were, in the void when the old forms have lost their quality of immediacy and transparency. Fifthly, they must be attuned not only to the Christian tradition but to the musical harmonies of the cosmos, expressing through them the eschatological joy that in some way is being anticipated in all fragments of the universe.

We should let the joy of our eschatological hope find new ways to celebrate the coming of the new world in new songs and new tongues. The liturgies of Christians should be miniature miracles of Pentecost on the way to perfect joy and love in the new world to come. Pentecost was a pluralistic happening. The ascetic spirit that rids worship of things to see and hear and smell and touch and taste is a curse especially on our Protestant tradition. If the Reformation succeeded in unstopping the ear so that the word of God could become an acoustical event, it also had the effect of shutting the eye and deadening the other senses. With liturgy having been so often bleak and dreary in Protestantism and so often archaistic in Roman Catholicism, we must welcome the present upsurge of interest in new forms of worship. The church must always be in quest of a new cult that is worthy of the newness of the gospel and the celebration of life in new forms. For the time being our liturgical life will seem chaotic and irregular, even messy and uneven. The Roman Catholic deacon who pulled off his shirt and danced down the aisle during the offertory, carrying the elements forward, was expressing the urge to celebrate the joy and mirth and freedom that the life in Christ makes possible. One could have predicted, of course, that he would be slapped down by his archbishop. And so many feel that they are being driven "underground" to find the freedom to worship according to their conscience, to express new vitalities of Pentecost that the institutionalized churches cannot accommodate—the ecstasy of joy, love toward strangers, unity with all mankind, and freedom to be open to new things. It may be that the pioneering work will have to be carried on in the "underground church," until enough pressure has been built up from below to force a change in the institutional churches. On the other hand, we perhaps need not be so pessimistic, because the institutional churches are showing here and there a surprising openness to change and willingness to sponsor sincere efforts to create new styles of worship.

II. THE LIMITS OF PLURALISM

So far we have uncovered a theological basis for pluralism in the church. It rests on her bipolar relation of openness to the future of God's Kingdom and openness to the world and its wealth of cultural forms. A static church will die by her refusal to be an open community. Every living church must experience a double conversion: to the Kingdom of God and to the world. But there can be no denying that there is a great risk for the church in being open to the world. The church has been warned by the apostle Paul: "Do not be conformed to this world" (Rom. 12:2). He warned against becoming "slaves to the elemental spirits of the universe" (Gal. 4:3) and against those who would make "a prey of you by philosophy and empty deceit, according to human tradition" (Col. 2:8). There are numerous similar warnings in the New Testament, and conservatives especially are fond of quoting them to scare church people from trying new things. The church at her best has known better than that. She has accepted the risk of being the church in the world, of taking the world into the church, and of baptizing it. She has affirmed the principle of the *complexio oppositorum*.[3] Knowing that life in the world is mixed with evil, the church has entered into all its dimensions, acting on the magna charta of Christian freedom: "For all things are yours," Paul says to the Corinthians (I Cor. 3:21). It doesn't matter who made it or where it comes from. Nothing that is created is off limits to Christians—nothing in nature, nothing in history, nothing in the country, nothing in the city, nothing in the past, nothing in the future. "All are yours; and you are Christ's; and Christ is God's." (Vs. 22–23.) It is especially the Roman Catholic Church that has accepted the risk of this kind of universality; it is symbolized in the great medieval cathedrals and in the great scholastic systems, which took into themselves samples of everything—from gargoyles to angels —to manifest the catholicity of the church's vision.

However, as long as the day of eschatological fulfillment has not yet arrived, the universality of the church is never fully actual. Catholicity is not a static predicate; it is a matter of mission, something to become more and more, and always still a thing of hope and anticipation. The church's universality is limited and must be limited by historical particularities, lest the church lose herself in the world before she reaches fulfillment in the Kingdom of God. In attempting to actualize her universality, the church is always risking her particularity. It is possible for a church to cease to be a church, to lose the gospel, to cool off by the loss of the Spirit's presence, to become secularized to the point of becoming nothing more than an imitation of the world. The church is always only one generation away from extinction. Each generation must transmit the tradition to the next. The threads of transmission are very fine. They can be snapped by misuse or disuse. The Christian church lives from a particular event of history and the irradiation of its eschatological character. That is in principle the only norm that limits the pluralism of the church. The Christian faith has a particular content. It makes a particular claim to truth, and that is that the all-fulfilling future of mankind and of the world's salvation has already arrived in its initial phase in Jesus, the Jew from Nazareth. Any church that ceases to affirm this event and to live out its meaning has ceased to be a Christian community.

There is no way to fix the limits of the church by asking about her circumference. There is no way of giving absolutely clear boundaries to the church. There is no way of fixing in advance the forms of belief and worship. And yet the church must draw the line against those isms which attack her foundations. The church must risk concrete decisions. No one would deny that the church may have been overly zealous in the past of spotting deviations and pronouncing her anathemas. On the other hand, a church that could not recognize the heresy of third-century Arianism or the apostasy of twentieth-century Aryanism would be too enfeebled to last another generation. And she would not deserve to last. Perhaps we could say that the church cannot set a priori limits to pluralism in doctrine and worship, but she must draw concrete lines a posteriori to beliefs and practices which violate the norm of her existence that is given in her very foundation in the Christ-happening. These lines can perhaps not be drawn once for all, but rather *ad hoc,* since the past decisions of the church have to be reviewed by each generation, to see if they also express adequately the faith of the church for her time.

Since creedal and liturgical expressions are always contextual, and only then meaningful, there is no core of doctrine or canon of the liturgy that has an unconditional and eternal validity in history. The norms that are derived from the Christ event are like the signals of a good quarterback; they can be changed at the line of scrimmage, depending on the formation of the enemy's defense. The derived norms that function in our doctrines and liturgies must be operational along the line of scrimmage where the church is today. The church does not have a tradition that she is merely supposed to sit on and keep warm; she does not have a truth to shut up inside as an oyster its pearl. She has a tradition and a truth to make her active as a missionary community on her way to the ends of the world until the end of time. (Matt. 28:19–20.) That is her apostolic commission, her reason for existence. This missionary vocation is an added source of pluralism. In carrying out this vocation, the church encounters other great religions.

She is faced with the task of making her own creeds and cults contextual, but the new context is permeated by pagan religion. For the church to win converts and to make headway in a foreign culture, she must make an enormous adjustment. She must be willing to risk some degree of syncretism, that is, blending her truth into the religious words and symbols of another culture. Some of the early church fathers thought of Christianity as the crowning fulfillment of the history of religions, the inclusive fullness of truth toward which all other religions were pointing as but partial realizations. In this way Christianity became the melting pot of the religions surrounding the Mediterranean basin. The inclusivist concept gave way to an exclusivist line in Western missionary ideology. According to this, Christianity is the true religion, fighting to displace all the false religions in the world. This idea of Christianity as the one and only saving religion helped to nourish the superiority attitudes and foster the empire-building ambitions of the white West. As if to compensate for this nightmare now, there are some Christians who have wearied of the missionary idea altogether, of whatever kind. They hesitate to admit that Christianity might have anything which could claim universal validity for all others. But this is a mistake. For the very being of the church is missionary; her very message as the announcement of the eschatological breakthrough in the historical event of Christ is inherently universally valid. And that means that the problem of syncretism, and the pluralism it engenders, is built into the missionary structure of the church.

The Western missions that followed the exclusivist line made the younger churches so shy of syncretism that they became ghettos for the preservation of the foreign syncretisms of the West. The history of Western Christianity is the story of the success and failure of syncretism. In a series of steps Christianity became Hellenistic, Byzantine, Roman, Germanic, Nordic, Anglo-Saxon, and American. It had to do so to make its message contextual and relevant to the particular culture in which it was proclaimed. Now if the younger churches in the new nations of the Third World operate on the model of the West, they must also become syncretistic. That is a risk, but it is also the only hope toward a true indigeneity. Perhaps they can even do a better job than the West, for the West can teach them something about false contextualization. A false indigeneity is one in which the church becomes excessively identified with the culture. Then the salt can lose its savor. Luther's protest was against an excessive "Romanizing" of Christianity, and he was right. The Confessional Church in Germany protested against an excessive "Aryanizing" of Christianity, and she was right. But these examples may not be used to frighten the younger churches from translating the faith into doctrines and rituals that bear the stamp of their own culture. Nothing is more frightful than the sight of a Ubangi tribe chanting its liturgy in Latin. A missionary cannot help transmitting the message with a large overspill of his own culture, but he seeks a new embodiment of the message in a culture that is still strange to the gospel.

The missionary church will lead the way in pushing back the limits of pluralism by using local concepts and symbols in building doctrine and local customs and sounds in the language of liturgy. So long as the daughter churches receive the "one thing needful" from the unbroken tradition of the church, they are free not to carry along all the baggage from the past—Jewish cult, Hellenistic philosophy, Roman law, Teutonic theology, and such things. They are free to plow their own furrows in history, and to bring all the things in their own culture into captivity to the obedience of Christ. (II Cor. 10:5.)

NOTES

1. Dietrich Bonhoeffer, "Protestantismus ohne Reformation," *Gesammelte Schriften*, ed. by Eberhard Bethge (Munich: Chr. Kaiser Verlag, 1958), Vol. I, p. 325.

2. Cf. Paul Tillich, *Systematic Theology* (*The University of Chicago Press*, 1963), Vol. III, pp. 196–201, where he discusses "the aesthetic function of the church."

3. *Ibid.*, p. 170.

V

THE EPISCOPATE
AND THE PETRINE OFFICE
AS EXPRESSIONS OF UNITY

Carl E. Braaten

INTRODUCTION

What new things can be said about the episcopate and the papal office at this time? And especially by a Protestant? On several previous occasions I have expressed the opinion that the reunited church of the future would be equipped with structures that retain some recognizable continuity with both papal and episcopal offices.[1] This sounded like a sellout to many Protestant theologians.[2] However, I balanced this prediction with a precondition, namely, that these offices themselves will pave the way for a new union of all Christian churches only when they sacrifice every authoritarian feature in theory and practice. It can hardly be said that any part of that precondition has been met by the hierarchical authorities. If anything, things have gone in the opposite direction. Whatever the morality of the case, the pope's position on the pill has turned into a struggle over authority. Bishop Francis Simons was not exaggerating when he said: "There is a growing revolt against the ecclesiastical teaching authority and traditional doctrines. Pope Paul is greatly worried." [3] The climate of feeling on authority has become very bad, not only in the church but in society generally, in politics, at the universities, and in family life. And the authorities have reacted by appealing to the traditional powers and prerogatives of their offices. So what new things can be said?

Theologians should not let the immediate church political situation, the behavior of bishops, or the pope's personality rob them of important gains they have made in advancing toward a theological consensus on the doctrine of the church. I believe that it is possible for Protestant and Catholic theologians to reach far-reaching agreement on the nature of the church, her mission, and ministry. I believe that this agreement is sufficient to draw us closer together in a common fellowship of worship and witness and action and not only in an underground movement. What I have to say will take the measure of the consensus that may be emerging among us. This does not mean that we will not be able to find differences, if we look for them. But an element of the consensus itself might be that these differences can be understood in such a way that they do not make all that much difference. Those who have a lot at stake in these differences might therefore accuse us of explaining them away. It will not be the first time a theologian has heard that accusation.

There are two main factors at work to reduce the differences between Catholics and Protestants. The first may be called the challenge of our historical origins and the second, the challenge of contemporary experience. It is by working together at these two poles of concern that theologians are closing the gaps between Christians today. Theologians who evade these two challenges hardly deserve to be called theologians; rather, they are ideologists who reiterate the confessional rhetoric that justifies their continued separation. They remain bound to the texts which were born in division. There is only so much reinterpretation that can be done from these texts. There is not enough hermeneutical skill on earth to get the texts which once inspired the age of polemics to serve now as documents of our reunion. The Lutheran Formula of Concord and the Roman Decrees of Trent can be reinterpreted only so far to accommodate the demands of our ecumenical age. What is required is a new input that is not exhausted by our rival confessional histories. The thesis of this address is that we now have a new input, first from the historical inquiry into our Christian origins and secondly from Christian participation in the revolutionary changes of our time.

I. THE CHALLENGE OF OUR HISTORICAL ORIGINS

First we shall propose what Protestants ought to acknowledge about the early origins of the Christian church. The old Protestant myth that there existed a consensus of the first five centuries (*consensus quinquesaecularis*), which the Reformation was only reinstating after the church had fallen into a millennium of dark ages, was exploded long ago by historical scholarship. Adolf von Harnack then moved the fall of the church back into the second century, when Christianity underwent what he called the process of hellenization. Catholics who have read Leslie Dewart's book, *The Future of Belief,* can easily get an inkling of what Harnack meant by the "hellenization of Christianity." But now some of our New Testament scholars are telling us that if we are going to speak of a "fall" of the church at all, it is something that occurred much earlier. The origins of early Catholicism can be traced right back into the New Testament itself.[4] If a radically spiritual (or existentialist) kind of Protestantism is the norm of what is authentically Christian, then the fall of the church is at least a second-generation, and not a second-century, occurrence. But to call the developments that took place a "fall" or an aberration from an originally pure Christianity is a value judgment that is not necessarily supported by the historical evidences. And there would hardly be a Protestant theologian who would carry out such a thesis without falling into extreme inconsistency. For one could show that his own Protestant faith is indebted to the very structures which he takes the liberty to criticize as "catholicizing" or "hellenizing," or even "paganizing." For example, the collection of books we call the New Testament, on at least a selection of which his faith is dependent, is a product of the church's attempt to fix certain limits to her tradition, to establish some norms. In doing so the church introduced a principle of order to balance the more spontaneous, free, and charismatic elements in her nature. It would be a strain on our common sense to call this sort of thing a "fall." If one is to operate with the hypothesis of a "fall" in a somewhat hyper-Protestant fashion, we are at the mercy of a purely arbitrary decision as to how far back we are willing to date it. Do we then go back as far as the apostle Paul himself?

I believe that most Protestant scholars would explain the transition from the apostolic to the postapostolic history of the church in terms of a creative historical development, rather than as a falling away from an originally pure Christianity. This development is historically instructive for us. First, it shows the amazing flexibility and versatility of the early communities to adjust to new situations. The paradox is that the early church used her freedom to create order. Secondly, we see that the guiding purpose in creating new orders was to serve the church's apostolicity. What the apostles had handed down was a treasury of Christ that should be preserved for the generations to come. Thirdly, new orders needed to be improvised to express the unity of the various communities within the ever-widening horizon of the church's missionary existence. To achieve universality without sacrificing unity was already a problem for the early church, and its solution, so far from being a degeneration, represented an astonishing degree of wisdom, faithfulness to the paradosis, and an innovating imagination that makes our modern period look sterile by comparison.

It is in the light of this daring freedom to create new instrumentalities to serve her fragile unity and apostolicity that the Protestant theologian ought to applaud the early development from the apostolic to the postapostolic history of the church. He can put a positive construction on the development of episcopacy, even the monarchical episcopacy; he can affirm the church's formation of a canon, creed, and cult. The church's eschatological message sent her on a mission whose every step increased her distance from the horizon of her apostolic origins. The message could be lost without the vehicles of transmission which the church created or borrowed from other religious communities, from the Old Testament or Hellenistic mystery cults. Catholics have always wanted to know by what logic Protestants pick and choose from among these vehicles of transmission, such as the canonical Scriptures, the ecumenical creeds, and the eucharistic liturgy. No two Protestant denominations agree on them. These are all mediums; they are not the message. But the same thing holds true of the episcopacy and the Petrine office. They are mediums; they are not the message. If the Protestant theologian accepts the canon, the creeds, and liturgies of the early church, there is no reason he cannot accept the offices which the early church created to cope with her needs on her missionary way. The most important question is not what offices, what orders, but what for? The challenge of our origins can help the Protestant theologian break the

habit of carrying sixteenth- or nineteenth-century preju-
dices back into second-century developments, dismissing
everything that smacks of later Catholicism as a perversion.

Similarly the challenge of our origins can have a liberating effect on Catholic theologians. I am yet unable to
tell whether it is harder for Catholic theologians to make
an honest response to this challenge than for Protestants.[5]
The first challenge is to acknowledge that what we have
called creative developments in second-century Christianity, what others call "catholicizing" or "hellenizing,"
were very early bolstered by historical fictions. We have
praised the early church for exercising her freedom to
innovate, to make changes, to try some new things. But the
trend set in to legitimate the new things by fictitiously de-
riving them from the past. The church became afraid of her
own freedom, and for this reason her new orders had to
be made constitutive of the church from the very beginning. And this was done by historical retrojection and by
creating historical fictions. Thus, the incipient catholic
orders in the pastoral epistles had somehow to be legitimated by "Paul." The need to strengthen the leadership
in the church to cope with heresies and enthusiasms that
broke out in the communities was met by the development
of the episcopal office, but the strength of this office was
inflated by the historical fiction of a chain of succession
that links up with Peter and the apostles. A similar fiction
was promoted by basing canonicity on apostolic author-
ship, for only a very small part of our New Testament can
be said to have been authored by any of the original
Twelve whom Jesus called to be his disciples. The title of
our apostolic creed is a somewhat less glaring example of
the same tendency to anoint the decisions of later times
with the unction of ancestral authorities. If we let our
minds run ahead into history, we will recall how similarly
the mystical writings of Pseudo-Dionysius and such for-

geries as the Donation of Constantine and the pseudo-Isidorian decretals made it possible to build massive and even monstrous systems of power and piety on the sands of historical fictions. The question the church had to face in time was whether she was willing to yield those powers and prerogatives that had been erected on fictions. The answer returned by history is that the church was never willing to yield any power until she was confronted by even greater power. And in the game of power politics the church has not been a winner in modern times. The lesson here might be that the church is being called upon now by the challenge of her origins to abandon all special status, every privileged position, all illusions of grandeur which the princes of the established churches claim for themselves. The structures of the church have given ultimate dogmatic sanction to the distortions which the twistings and turnings of history brought about. And so the ecclesiastic offices have been thought of as powers that rule from above; office-holders as dignitaries who are conscious of rank and diplomatic immunities; ordinary laymen as subjects whose most cherished virtue is obedience to the higher authorities and leading a quiet and peaceful life in the world.

I am not telling Catholic theologians to take seriously the challenge of our origins; they are already doing that. It will take some time, as it always does, for the power of the knowledge of this truth to trickle down to the hierarchy. What a radically different vision of the church we find, for example, in those Catholic authors who let the historical origins speak for themselves, rather than stand as a mere legitimation for the ecclesiastical dogmas of later centuries. Why should not these earlier origins be more important than those later dogmas, since the dogmas of the church can never stand on their own legs, but require for their support the history that is inherent in the foundations of the church.

We agree on how zealous the church was and must be in anchoring herself in what the apostles handed down. The continuing life of the church depends on what the apostles transmitted as the first witnesses. Apostolicity is of the essence of the church. It is not surprising then that the church would take great care to see that the apostolic witness would have a future in history. The apostles can have no successors in a literal sense. The role of the original witness or receiver of revelation cannot be transferred. But there must be an apostolic succession, a succession of apostolic faith and obedience, of the apostolic message and mission. And it is not only not improper but inevitable that agencies be developed to tend to this concern—to be servants of apostolicity. This function becomes localized in an office. This office can be a servant and sign of the true apostolic succession.

A possible consensus breaks into dissensus when this ecclesiastical office acts as though it has a monopoly on the apostolic succession, when it thinks in terms of guarantees, a priori authority, and dominion from above. Then the very offices that ought to serve the unity of the church by submitting themselves to its apostolicity become the instruments which divide the church. The episcopal and Petrine offices may be legitimated as instruments and expressions of unity. However, they become the cause of division, and this I think is historically demonstrable, when either or both of two things happen: (1) when the spirit of service as shown by our Lord is exchanged for the appetite to rule over the church like a secular prince and (2) when the powers and privileges acquired by these offices in the vacuums of political history become retroactively inscribed by dogma into the original constitution of the church.

II. THE DYNAMICS OF OUR
PRESENT SITUATION

Not only the challenge of our origins but also the dynamics of modern experience invite us to deal dialectically with the episcopal and Petrine offices, to say both "yes" and "no." We can say "yes" to what they ought to be, in view of the continuing needs of the church for *servants* and *signs* of that unity which defines true apostolic succession. We can say "yes" to the achievements of these offices in caring for the unity of the church, in symbolizing the universality of the mission, in focusing on the apostolicity of the ministry. We do not need to blind ourselves either to the cultural services of these offices, to their political contributions, to their concerns for public morality, for in extending her voice and influence outside her own walls, the church is bearing witness that she exists for the whole of humanity, that she has a light to bring to the nations, and carries within herself prefigurations of the future that is in store for all mankind. These offices can be concrete symbols of the historicality of the church as a visible phenomenon in space and time. She not only has her own history; she is there to make new history, by releasing her energies of love and projecting her images of hope into the open field of world history. These offices are, indeed, evidences of the church's institutionalization, but it is sheer enthusiasm to think of the church as an invisible phenomenon, as an event without social embodiment, as merely a name for a certain kind of fugitive existential experience. The early church created these offices to mobilize herself against the world-denying and history-evading tendencies of gnosticism. Today, these offices may help the church to stick to history, to resist the temptation to drop

out, and to desert our stations at the front line of history
where the new things of God are wrought through struggle,
through suffering, and through service. Each individual
Christian may surely be free "to do his own thing." But
we need the kinds of offices that remind us and tell us that
we are to be together, to do things together, that we have a
unity, a common mission, a shared memory that goes far
back and a vision that reaches way ahead, embracing all
separated individuals in the final rendezvous of mankind
in the coming Kingdom of God. Now, if we did not already
have offices in the church to assume these necessary tasks,
we would have to create them. We would surely have to
watch lest they claim too much for themselves, lest they
inflate what is historically relative into something dog-
matically absolute. We have to decide whether we should
kill what we have, wipe the slate of history clean, and start
all over with brand-new offices that can serve the troops.
Then we would be total revolutionaries who dream of an
absolutely new beginning with no hold on our past. Or we
may try to change what we have, to increase the pressures
for reform and renewal, to reorient the offices away from
the hierarchical model toward the image of the servant.
Then we may be anything from mild revisionists to radical
reformers, but we will recognize that the dream of total
revolutionaries is not only anarchistic but also a foolish
illusion that plays into the hands of the extreme conservatives who do not want anything to change. If you ask for
everything all at once, you end by getting nothing—that
happens with such regularity in our human experience, we
can even call it a law. On the basis of the hope for radical
reform, we can envision a church of the future in which
the episcopate and the Petrine office really function as
signs and servants of essential dimensions of the church.
We can say "yes" to them from out of our Protestant experience, insofar as without them we have learned that our

unity can be degraded into uniformity. Nothing is more boring than the sameness that is cultivated within a Protestant denomination—sameness in piety, sameness in ethical code, sameness in polity, sameness in doctrine, etc. In addition to this, the diversities between Protestants, taken together with blue-ribbon claims to uniqueness and superiority advanced by each one, have resulted in a loss of catholic identity. Each one narrows its claim to uniqueness to the point it cuts itself off as a sect, confusing its members about their essential relation to the international community of Christ. For example, I was brought up in the Norwegian Lutheran Church in America. The doctrine was Lutheran, the piety was Norwegian, the culture was American—all of which could be mixed together to conceal the priority of the church's international identity. We do not want less diversity than Protestants have, but we do not want these diversities to deny our unity and to overshadow our identity. So it may be that Protestants will be willing to affirm the episcopal and Petrine offices under new conditions that, first of all, promise to make up for a lack they have experienced, and secondly, represent a radical recasting in line with the cultural dynamics of our present historical situation.

Why is such a recasting necessary? It is not only necessary to do this to please Protestants and to take care of the objections they have legitimately been making; it is not only necessary to do this to win the respect of modern man who has developed a sense of autonomy that he will never sacrifice to the Grand Inquisitors of religion or politics; it is necessary to do this for the sake of those who are already faithful sons of the Roman Catholic Church. They too have been challenged by their origins; they too are modern men, and thus culturally indisposed to accept final authorities, absolute principles, inerrant documents, and infallible offices during this interim of waiting with hope and striving in history for the finality of God's future that still lies ahead of us. They too wish to participate in the decisions that affect their lives. They too are suspicious of oracles that are voiced from above, of decisions made behind closed doors, of actions that rest on official fiat. I do not believe that the church can ignore the dynamics of history with impunity. She has never yet succeeded in doing this. The dynamic forces of historical destiny may be driven underground for a time, but they will surface again, taking a heavy toll on those who put up the most relentless opposition. In a facetious remark on TV, I heard the editor of the *National Catholic Reporter* quote the saying that is making the rounds, that while Pope John opened the windows in the church, his successor is opening the doors. Maybe that is a way of stating that a radical recasting of the church's image of authority is needed, not, as I said, to please Protestants but as a truly catholic response to the demands of freedom and the rights of conscience. It may be that the decisions that must be made cannot follow the wishes of a few on top, but must be dictated by the needs of the needy below. A church must be defended against the personal hang-ups of those who have a need to rule over others and to make others into carbon copies of themselves. The church has had such leaders in the past, and her present episcopal and papal structures and modes of operation still make it possible, even likely. I do not think the church can get away with it any longer. There are too many pressures from the gospel against it, and the deepest tendencies of man in our age are in open rebellion against authoritarian systems of control. So why should the church persist in hanging on to an anachronism?

It was not anachronistic but historically understandable that the Petrine office would—chameleon-like—take on characteristics of Roman law and politics, that the Western church would develop along juridical lines, that the power of the pope would increase immeasurably with the collapse of the empire, that notions about hierarchy, succession, centralism, and absolutism would be transferred from the secular imperium to the ecclesiastic magisterium, and that the magisterium would itself become mainly a power structure, an "administerium." [6] The history is there for everyone to see. The urgent question is whether the Petrine office will now open itself as radically to modernization as once it did to the process of Romanization. If the Roman Catholic Church was once free to become so thoroughly Roman, why should she not now claim the same freedom to become thoroughly modern? For once upon a time, to be modern was to be Roman. But not any more!

No Christian has a right to confess his faith in the one, holy, *Roman* Church. That would be sectarian—as for a church to call herself Lutheran in some other sense than as a provisional expedient, we might even say, as an accident of church history. Her Romanism is not an essential dimension of the constitution of the church. By undertaking a thoroughgoing de-Romanization of her governing structures, it will appear to many traditionalists that the church is committing an act of self-demolition. It is hard for our imagination to grasp what the papacy will look like and act like when it becomes a ministry in the church, of the church, and for the church, when it becomes reborn in the image of the servant of Christ. Long before Pope John's example, long before the Reformation, Joachim of Floris and the Franciscans had a prophetic dream that envisioned a future transformation of the hierarchical church into the *ecclesia spiritualis*[7] and a conversion of the authoritarian model of papal power into the service of a *papa angelica*, an angelic pope, who would represent the present of the Spirit in a theonomous way. That is a dream that is being renewed within the church today.

CONCLUSION

How much of that dream can we realistically expect to see fulfilled in the not-too-distant future? The most lucid thing we can state is that a good measure of that dream will have to be fulfilled before the hierarchical structure of the church will cease to be the most glaring symbol of our disunity, before the episcopate and the Petrine office can be expressions of unity. As a conclusion I am going to offer a few glimpses of what that dream might mean. Marshall McLuhan has called our attention to our passing from an age of mechanization into an electronic age. And that has certain implications for our life together as human beings, as Christians and servants of a community. "As anything becomes more complex, it becomes less specialized." [8] We are moving away from the age of specialization, which dealt with the problem of complexity by dividing up the whole community into a number of parts, and assigning a specialized function to each. Bishops and popes were assigned the functions of passing on authoritative information and exercising authoritative government. In other words, their primary specialized functions in the religious community were as magisterium and administerium. The question is whether the electronic age will not render these specialized roles somewhat obsolete. We must reckon with a prior anachronism that existed in the mechanical age when we asked bishops to be discerners of correct doctrine, when that function had long since been transferred to theologians. It is an anachronism to ask bishops to be the experts in the interpretation of Scripture, when this presupposes the most sophisticated disciplines of historical understanding. The cultural basis of magisterial authority was shattered by the explosion of knowledge and modern intellectual specialization, so that what remained was chiefly the doctrinal claim hanging by a thin thread from above. Such a doctrinal claim, delivered from on high, without grounding in the cultural situation is felt to be authoritarian, and finally antihuman. The mere repetition or hardening of the claim to authority does not close the gap. But now, Marshall McLuhan tells us, the centuries of explosion are being followed by electric implosion. "The electronic age is literally one of illumination. Just as light is at once energy and information, so electric automation unites production, consumption, and learning in an inextricable process." [9] Electric implosion will mean total interdependence. And this will mean that men are interrelated as never before, involved together in the total social process as never before, becoming more and more one tribe in one world. The old idea that there are elite groups who are in the know and have the right to rule must fall away with the withering of fragmentary specialization of the mechanical age.

Still, however, our new society will need the ministry of Christ and the ministries of the church. And among those ministries we can imagine that certain traditional forms, like episcopacy and the Petrine office, will be manifest and function in new ways. When they get rid of their authoritarian and triumphalist habits from the past, and take on the form of the servant, they will become a "cool medium." [10] McLuhan defines this as "high in participation or completion by the audience." [11] The institutional church has traditionally relied on "hot" media. The statements of ecclesiastical authorities and church commissions are usually of this kind, for they are low in participation and in completion by the audience. Not only the world yawns, but church members are lulled to sleep by these one-way declarations of monological media. Christian leaders, the gurus of our community, will speak with authority no longer from the pinnacle of a pyramid. They will speak from the valleys of experience, with improvised actions along the caravan trail of our nomadic existence. They will speak by a gesture here, through a parable there. The medium will be "cool." Jesus was a "cool" medium, for though he was in the form of God, he did not cling to that almighty medium, and speak and act from outside the field, but he emptied himself, taking the form of the servant, entering into the field, in humility and obedience, all the way to death. Why should his disciples and apostles, and their successors to the present time, ask for an easier authority, an exalted form, a "hot" medium outside the field? How can they be lords already, and not always servants? What has changed to allow the servant of Christ to be known more by his "highness" than by his humility? Jesus proclaimed the Kingdom in parables. And parables are a "cool" medium, for they arise from a situation in which the speaker is involved together with his hearers. The parable begins with participation, and in that situation a disclosure occurs, and this disclosure effects a demand. So the demand follows upon disclosure, and disclosure upon a sharing of speaker and audience in a life situation. And the new things that happen are not dictations from above that have to be obeyed in a legalistic manner, that are valid merely because of "who says so." The new things arise from the truth of the parable, because the parable brings the power of God's Kingdom into alliance with the everyday things of life.[12]

It seems to me that any new validation of the episcopal and Petrine offices, or any other offices in the church, must not be content with the roles and rationalizations assigned to them from the past. To be valid they must be just as much questioned by our present, and also oriented to the future. For if they were merely faithful to the past, while blocking out the future, they would be enemies of mankind and bad instruments of the gospel. For the gospel is what opens the future, the future for man on the basis of the arrival of God's future in the Jew from Palestine. The servants of the people of God are to be signs that point to the future: they have an eschatological orientation. If they do not have that, they have nothing at all to do with Christianity. They will be known by their parables and not by their definitions; they will be effective at the point of participation, not through lofty declarations.

As servants of the exodus people the leaders will keep their missionary identity alive by keeping the story of their destiny lively. If we may refer to McLuhan again, he tells us that the new electronic age will result in "retribalization." But the new tribe of the world needs a story. Psychological experiments have shown that if a man is deprived of his memory of the past, he is completely immobilized. The traditional offices of leadership in the church must project the story of the tribe; these offices may be symbols of continuity, of a historical succession of a common faith, a common obedience, a common pilgrimage. As a Lutheran Christian, I do not want to see these offices wither away. I hope for their renewal through the challenge of our origins, and in response to the needs of this coming age. In the total field of the electromagnetic interprocess, as McLuhan envisions it, the tasks that our *episcopoi* must do will be not to give information—computers will do that—but to use their imagination; not to rule—we all will participate in that—but to act out the story with significant actions, like a Martin Luther King, Jr., sitting in a Birmingham jail, like a Eugene Carson Blake getting arrested on a demonstration, like a Benjamin Spock being put on trial for subversive activities. In the future our bishops will do such things as parables of the Kingdom. They will have the authority of the parable, spoken from participation in the everyday situation into which the power of God's Kingdom breaks from the future. This is a dream of the future. The realization of this dream will coincide with the reunion of the divided churches; it will signal the recovery of prophecy in the church, a new outpouring of the Spirit, a new zeal for world mission, a deeper experience of unifying love. Although all that sounds utopian, we can hardly imagine that the genuine objects of Christian hope for our time can be spelled out in lesser terms.

NOTES

1. Cf. "The Reunited Church of the Future," *Journal of Ecumenical Studies,* Vol. 4, No. 4 (1967), pp. 611–628; "Rome, Reformation, and Reunion," *Una Sancta,* Vol. 23, No. 2 (1966), pp. 3–8.

2. For example, Kyle Haselden, editor of *The Christian Century,* who wrote several editorials, entitled "Protestant Hara-Kiri" (June 22, 1966) and "The Braaten Brouhaha" (Oct. 26, 1966).

3. Francis Simons, *Infallibility and the Evidence* (Templegate, Publishers, 1968), p. 120.

4. Ernst Käsemann, "Paulus und der Frühkatholizismus," *Exegetische Versuche und Besinnungen* (Göttingen: Vandenhoeck & Ruprecht, 1964), Vol. II.

5. Hans Küng's latest book, *The Church* (Sheed & Ward, Inc., 1968), is an example of what I would call an honest response.

6. Simons, *op. cit.,* p. 119.

7. See the book on Joachim of Floris, by Ernst Benz, *Ecclesia Spiritualis* (Stuttgart: W. Kohlhammer Verlag, 1964).

8. I am indebted for this McLuhanism (and to some of the others that follow) to a friend of mine, Jerome Nilssen, who quotes it in an unpublished paper he wrote for a study commission of the Lutheran Church in America. The paper

was entitled "The Minister: His Role and His Self-Image."
The quotation comes from *Understanding Media* (McGraw-
Hill Book Company, Inc., 1964), p. 309.

9. *Ibid.,* p. 304.

10. *Ibid.,* p. 36.

11. *Ibid.*

12. See Wolfhart Pannenberg, *Jesus—God and Man,* tr. by
Lewis L. Wilkins and Duane A. Priebe (The Westminster
Press, 1968), p. 231.

VI

THE CHURCH
AND
THE ESCHATOLOGICAL
KINGDOM

Wolfhart Pannenberg

IN the Protestant tradition, the church has been widely understood as a congregation of the faithful (*congregatio fidelium*). Perhaps this idea gives a fairly accurate sociological description of the religious community from which all more complex ecclesiastical institutions have developed. And in some broader sense even the big confessional churches may be characterized as congregations of individual believers, whatsoever the institutional form of these churches may be. On the other hand, this description does not tell what the church is all about. It does not express the purpose of this organization, the reason for its existence. In the traditional Lutheran formula that distinctive nature of the church is referred to as pure doctrine and correct administration of the sacraments. But this phrase is no longer particularly satisfying, since not only the criteria but even the possibility of pure doctrine in the sense of the sixteenth century has become problematic. For the discussion approaching a new definition of the nature of the church, I want to contribute some remarks about what should be the leading perspective of any such attempt: the nature and the purpose of the church cannot be adequately dealt with except in relation to the Kingdom of God.

This is not a self-evident statement. It is not common to take the Kingdom of God as the basis for a doctrine of the church. One reason for this may be an unawareness of the difference between the church and the Kingdom. Many are accustomed to think about God's Kingdom only in connection with the end of history, while the time of the church is the time of human pilgrimage in this world. The Kingdom of God, then, becomes a special subject for the last chapter of human history and of Christian dogmatics, although the Kingdom of the one God should concern everything even in the present world and in past ages. If the Kingdom of God is understood to be "eschatological" in the peculiar sense of being restricted to the last period of history, then the church as a reality of the present age has to be explained by different principles than eschatology. Therefore, it is understandable that the description of the church as the bride of Christ or the body of Christ has been more familiar in theology than the connection of church and Kingdom. If the church is conceived as the body of Christ, her purpose can be recognized in the mission to spread the gospel about Jesus Christ among all people, to unite all people within the church, and to preserve the Christians in unity with Christ. Such a description is not wrong. There is nothing to object against it, except that it needs further clarification.

Precisely at this point the idea of the Kingdom must enter the discussion. The title "Christ" was rooted in the Jewish expectation of the Kingdom of God. Therefore the description of the church as bride of Christ or body of Christ is also related to the divine Kingdom which has been made present by the Christ. In this perspective, however, unity with Christ is no longer a private relationship with Jesus, but is connected with the purposes of God concerning all mankind. These purposes of God's Kingdom, however, are not confined to the well-being and increase of the church. Correspondingly, communion with Christ is not yet achieved by formal adherence to the Christian community nor by sacramental communion alone, unless there is participation in the Kingdom of God, which according to Jesus, is presently at work through love. Sacramental communion in its true sense imports that the participants are opened up for the universal concerns of the one God who is the father of all men and whose presence Jesus proclaimed, whose communion we seek in the sacrament.

The gospel spread by the apostles did not only report remarkable and memorable events of the past which gave rise to the Christian tradition and to the Christian church, but the decisive point was that in those events the Kingdom of God had erupted into human history—the same reality which still is the ultimate future of the world and which only began in Jesus Christ. Since that future has become apparent in him, the history of Christ bears incomparable importance for all mankind. It gives the clue to fully participate in the ultimate destiny of mankind now. This is the substance and the urgency of the apostolic gospel. The action of spreading the gospel is related to the ultimate future of those to whom the gospel is proclaimed. It does not only report past events, but the history it reports illuminates the future of any audience, because it tells of the destiny of the human race, and hence it illuminates every present situation and throws back its light over all history.

Thus the mission of the church is related to the future of the Kingdom of God. The proclamation of the gospel continues the message of Jesus himself announcing the imminent Kingdom of God. Therefore, as the apostolic mission was constitutive for the church, so is the Kingdom of God that had become present in the Christ whom the apostles proclaimed. The anticipation of the Kingdom of God was not only the center in Jesus' teaching. It also determines the universal relevance of his history. It therefore explains the drive toward universal mission which characterizes Christianity since the days of Paul. Thus the Kingdom is not only the ultimate goal of the church. It has been present at her origin, continuously motivating and animating her mission. It is the origin of the church because it has been anticipated in the history of Christ. It is the goal of the church because of the Christian hope for future consummation of the church's communion with Christ. Thus the Kingdom of God offers the most comprehensive answer to the question about the reason and purpose of the Christian congregation. Even the fact that individual Christians cannot keep their new life in isolation for private enjoyment, but get together in congregations, indicates an aspect of the Kingdom, the social character of the Kingdom of God which will accomplish the perfection of the social destiny of man in peace and justice.

The idea of the Kingdom of God is related to the church as the people of God. And it offers also a corrective to that conception of the church. For the Kingdom of God is certainly universal. The power of the one God cannot be conceived as limited to certain areas. It extends to the whole world and to every individual. Hence the church while being particular cannot be the people of God in a restrictive sense, but only as representing all mankind by pioneering a unity of the entire human race that hitherto doesn't yet exist.

A full-range treatment of the doctrine of the church in the perspective suggested by the idea of the divine Kingdom is beyond the scope of this lecture. The discussion

112 SPIRIT, FAITH, AND CHURCH

must be limited to a few aspects of the problem. The three aspects I have selected are the apostolicity and catholicity of the church and her relation to the political community. These three aspects seem particularly convenient for a judgment about the relevance of such a conception of the church, and on the other hand they bear special importance for the ecumenical dialogue and for the situation of Christianity in the modern world.

1. *Apostolicity:* THE CHURCH ON THE ROUTE TOWARD THE KINGDOM

The very basis of the mission of the apostles, originating in the appearances of the risen Christ was the presence in himself of the eschatological glory of the Kingdom of God that Jesus had announced. The new and imperishable life of the risen one was nothing else than the glory of God's Kingdom manifested with Jesus. This was of concern to every human being, not only to the Jewish people, because it was the goal and end of all human history which had become apparent in Jesus and which was to be shared by all men. Thus the proclamation of God's act in Christ aiming at the salvation of all mankind went out to all the peoples of the ancient world. It was Paul's understanding that he had to proclaim this message in every place on earth before the Kingdom of God would finally come in power. The chance to participate in the future glory was to be opened up to everybody before God would come to judgment over his enemies.

Thus the apostolic mission started from the experience of the presence of God's universal salvation in Christ and went accordingly to all peoples, and in this it was facing the imminence of God's final Kingdom. The future of God's Kingdom was the point of orientation for the self-understanding of the apostles.

But soon the church founded by the apostles looked back to the apostolic age as to the classic and normative age of the church. The orientation toward the future was replaced by an orientation toward the past, contrary to the thrust of the apostolic mission itself. The endeavor was to preserve what the church had inherited from the apostles, preserve it without any change. Apostolic doctrine, apostolic life, apostolic office of the church were conceived of as identical with the ideal forms of the apostolic age. The changes which in fact happened in the course of the history of the church were suppressed in her self-consciousness. But there emerged different conceptions of what was considered truly apostolic. Each side blamed the other for having changed the apostolic heritage. But both lived in the illusion of preserving unchanged the apostolic forms of Christian life and doctrine.

The self-understanding of the churches, therefore, was seriously challenged by the discovery of historical development in modern times. To many it seemed as if the apostolic substance was being lost in the process of change. But perhaps this trouble did only reflect an inappropriate conception of apostolicity. It would be more true to the self-understanding of the apostles if we would conceive the apostolicity of the church in terms of her *mission* to all humanity. From this perspective, change is even necessary, for the church has to bear witness to the universal and ultimate salvation which happened in Christ under changing conditions and in different situations of different societies and cultures and in different periods of human history. To proclaim the ultimate truth as revealed in Jesus in the context of new experience requires change of earlier formulations which may have been adequate for earlier experience. And above all the mission of the apostles which has been passed over to the church (since it cannot come to an end until the consummation of history) is directed to the future of God's Kingdom. This future brings about change for every present situation.

Thus apostolicity is no longer opposed to historical change. To the contrary, it necessitates change and represents the criterion for discernment of those changes which are demanded from those which are not. The apostolic church is a church in movement into an open future greater than herself, the future of God's Kingdom which can bring salvation instead of judgment to all men. It is this aim that the apostolic church is serving and promoting.

2. *Catholicity:* AN EXAMPLE FOR THE PRESENCE OF THE KINGDOM

Although the term "catholic" was introduced into the Christian language not before the second century, there is a substantial connection between the confession to the catholicity of the Christian church and the universality of the Kingdom of God. Perhaps the best justification of the idea of the church's catholicity is offered in the prospect that the Kingdom of God will comprise all mankind.

There are, of course, alternative ways to justify the idea of a catholic, i.e., universal church. The most serious alternative is offered by reference to the undivided unity of the body of Christ: this unity excludes the idea of separate churches opposing and repudiating each other; it rather requires universal communion among all Christian groups and congregations. But the idea of catholicity includes elements beyond that. It has often been forgotten, but it was mentioned already by Cyril of Jerusalem and has been emphasized again by the Second Vatican Council that the catholicity of the church is related not only to Christian unity but also to the unity of mankind beyond the limits of the church. This cannot be justified adequately by hypotheses built upon the identity of human nature as inherited by all individuals, but rather by reference to the future destiny of mankind, to the universal Kingdom of God which first makes the unity of human nature an element of Christian theology and, especially, of ecclesiology.

The distinctive point in the idea of the catholicity of the church, beyond that of Christian unity, immediately entails that the predicate of catholicity belongs to the church precisely in her self-transcendence. No church is catholic when taken as a limited community—as every church is regarding the numbers of membership and the peculiarities of tradition and institutional order. Christian communities and individual Christians can be catholic only by transcending the limitations of their own situation, of their form of life and of their measure of understanding acquired so far. The predicate of catholicity is always related to the eschatological fullness of the church in contrast to the limitations of particular phases of her self-realization in history. The eschatological fullness indicated by the idea of catholicity coincides with the Kingdom of God. But God's Kingdom is beyond the limitations of each historical realization of Christian community. Thus the Kingdom of God differs from the church during her pilgrimage through history. There is no justification for the church to be identified with the Kingdom, not even with the Kingdom of Christ, which Augustine thought embodied in the church. The provisional character of every realization of Christian life at present easily escapes from Christian thought, when the fundamental difference between church and Kingdom is forgotten. But on the other hand, the church of Christ is related to the eschatological fullness of the Kingdom of God. It is the goal of her mission, of her desires and prayers.

In some way the church already participates in this goal beyond herself, beyond the limitations of her respective historical situations. Precisely this comes to expression in the idea of catholicity. Catholicity designates the way in which the Kingdom is present in the church, but also in the life of individual believers, although it is still different from both because of the limitations of their present participation in the divine spirit. With other words, catholicity points to the possibility of individual Christians and particular Christian communities to participate in the Kingdom of God now, in spite of the limitations of their present reality, in a spirit of humility and openness beyond those limitations.

It is necessary to consider a little bit more closely the general structure of this openness in order to find out some of the conditions of genuine catholicity. The full dynamic of this idea comes into focus when one realizes that the idea of a catholic church comprises not only Christian communities from distant places on earth but also the Christian communities of different periods of Christian history, not only in the past, but also in the future. Openness beyond the limitations of one's own historical situation means, then, not only sympathy with contemporary Christian communities in other continents and of different cultures but also concern for the entire history of Christianity, not just for the traditions of one's own denomination. And the desire to be fair to and to concur with the truth in different strands of Christian tradition must not prevent an openness for future developments and possibilities of Christianity and for human needs which Christianity must meet. It is at this point that the concern for the human situation in general, especially in those aspects which have not yet been integrated into the Christian community and tradition, belongs to the logic of catholicity.

No particular Christian denomination should exclusively claim catholicity for its own particular tradition and institutional order in distinction from others. Particularity always imports limitation. Therefore, nothing particular as such can be catholic. On the other hand, no particular Christian community is a priori excluded from possible participation in the catholic nature of the church, according to the degree of its openness beyond the limitations of its own traditions in doctrine and institutional order. Particularity and catholicity are not mutually exclusive, on the condition that the particular remains open for the still more comprehensive universality of truth. In this sense not only a community but also individual Christians can embody catholicity. In every event, however, it requires the modest and humble awareness of the distance of one's own tradition, doctrine, and form of life from the eschatological fullness of the truth to be revealed in the future of God's Kingdom. Genuine catholicity, therefore, excludes all claims to uniformity, not only in matters of liturgy and discipline but also in doctrine. True catholicity is consistent with pluriformity in all these fields. Here the fundamental ecumenical importance of catholicity becomes apparent. The unity it invokes is the unity of spirit in the midst of pluriformity, and the unity of spirit can emerge only when every attempt is avoided to impose uniformity.

The distinction made in this argument between the limited character of every historical situation and the eschatological fullness of catholicity, which marks the determination of the church, is now received in faith and will be fully accomplished and revealed in the future of God's Kingdom. This distinction is intended to replace the distinction between visible and invisible church, so familiar and, at the same time, so disturbing in Protestant discussions of the nature of the church.

The true catholic church is not simply invisible at present, but can be embodied in communities and even in individual Christians, if they only open themselves beyond the limitations of their own particularities for the riches of the divine spirit according to the wide dimensions of

God's Kingdom. Thus the humble awareness of the difference between the church and the Kingdom, between one's
own provisional form of life and knowledge and the ultimate truth, is the decisive condition for that difference to
be overcome, i.e., for the presence of the divine spirit and
thus of the Kingdom of God in the midst of our perishable
and recusant lives, which remain at their best a fragment
of the divine glory promised to them. Strangely enough,
the catholic spirit withdraws from Christian communities
and individuals when and wherever they claim to possess
catholicity in definite form. This experience confirms once
more the ecstatic, spiritual character of the catholicity of
the church and of the presence of the Kingdom. Therefore, it should not weaken, but encourage the effort to let
the spiritual unity among Christians become increasingly
more visible in our time.

3. THE POLITICAL CHARACTER OF THE KINGDOM
AND THE FUNCTION OF THE CHURCH IN THE SOCIETY

The last subject earlier selected in order to illustrate the
relevance of the Kingdom of God as point of view for a
doctrine of the church is not foreign from the idea of
catholicity. A specific element in this idea was the concern
of the church beyond the Christian community for humanity and human life outside the walls of the religious organization of the church. The universal character of the
church depends on how comprehensive the Christian vision
proves to be regarding the problems of human existence.
One aspect of this is the social and political condition of
human existence—an important aspect for men of all
times, but especially in our days, when the subjection of
nature by men has been achieved to a remarkable degree,
but at the price of the emergence in social life of repressive

and alienating structures and tendencies which so far have not yet been brought sufficiently under control.

In the perspective of the Kingdom, the existence of the church cannot be understood as an end in itself. The existence of such an institution is justified only by the service that the church renders to the basic concerns of mankind. And especially it is the political destiny of man in relation to which the function of the church must be considered. This is so because the idea of the Kingdom of the Biblical God clearly has a political origin and political substance. In Isaiah's vision it was God who was the only true king, the sovereign of Israel and of the world, while the kings of Jerusalem only represented God's kingship on earth. According to the later prophets this earthly representation of God's Kingdom passed into the hands of the Babylonian empire, when Jerusalem was captured by Nebuchadnezzar, and later it was given to the Persian kings and after their period to the successors of Alexander. But already in the days of the Jewish kings it was felt that in their reign the Kingdom of Yahweh didn't come to full vigor. Hence the perfect realization of God's Kingdom was expected from the future. It would accomplish definitely what the human kings failed to achieve: universal peace and justice according to the law that was given to Moses.

Thus from the beginning the hope for the Kingdom of God has had a strong political note. This remains true in the later tradition, although the apocalyptic writers found it difficult to imagine a definite state of peace and justice in the present world among people as they now are. Therefore they postulated a fundamental change in the structure of creation and of human existence. They envisaged a new creation and the resurrection of the dead, as concomitant to if not precondition of the definite victory of the Kingdom of God.

In apocalyptic thought one can find a tendency to give

the hope for the Kingdom a more transcendental tinge. But still, if one turns to Jesus and considers the political character of the hope for God's Kingdom, it remains a riddle, how in Jesus' message this idea could occupy the central place without leaving the faintest impression of its political bearing. Suppose we would not know from the Old Testament about the political implications of the hope for God's Kingdom, it would be hard to discover this in the New Testament writings. Although the term itself remains a political metaphor, it is understandable that the Christian message could be interpreted in a thoroughly nonpolitical way. But then the core of the problem escapes us as to how the political hope for God's Kingdom could possibly take on such a nonpolitical appearance as it in fact did in the message of Jesus.

Obviously the answer to this question bears far-reaching consequences for the self-understanding of the church in both her connection with and distance from political life. Perhaps the most appropriate solution is that it was precisely the political reality of the Kingdom of God that entered this world by the private calling on individuals in Jesus' message and by the proclamation of individual salvation in early Christianity. If that is correct, it has taken a long time until the political relevance of the religious individualism of early Christianity penetrated the political structures of the societies formed by Christian peoples. It got through when Christians, encouraged by their communion with Christ in faith, felt themselves authorized to govern themselves because they participated in the kingship of Christ.

External and technical changes in the institutional structures of social life cannot solve, as many believe today, fundamental problems of human existence such as selfishness and ambition or acedia and faintheartedness. But the endowment of individuals with the freedom of faith in a community stimulated by concern for each other and for all fellowmen, must finally penetrate to the level of social and political action. Modern discussions on democracy are not always aware of the fact that the freedom and equality of all citizens, presupposed in democratic procedures, must first be accomplished again and again. Neither equal freedom nor that precious sense of public responsibility belongs to the natural equipment every individual was born with. They first have to be provided, and the most efficient agency working in this field has been—in spite of all its shortcomings and serious limitations—the Christian churches, the spirit communicated by Christian tradition.

Here the church is entrusted with an important educational function in the context of modern political life. This does not imply that the Kingdom of God could be established in the world by the educational efforts of Christianity. Such an assumption would disregard not only the cruel lessons of our century but also the more general wisdom, that every model of social life and institutions has its own unexpected but unavoidable limitations and even perversions. Nevertheless it remains true that the Kingdom of God is intended to become present, if only in provisional ways, in relevant forms of peace and justice among men. Thus there is—and must continue—a positive influence of Christian spirit in political life.

This argument would be mistaken, if one would conclude that the church should dissolute herself into a transformed, a Christianized culture. The continuous existence of the church as a separate, religious community besides the political structure of the society is required as long as the Kingdom of God is not yet definitely realized in political life. In this point the Marxist theory is right: religion owes its continuous persistence only to the inadequacy of the social realization of human destiny. In the perfect society of the future there will be no need any more for religion. Similarly the apocalypsis of John said that in the Kingdom of God, in the new Jerusalem, there will be no temple. The only question is, whether any socialist or communist construction of the society definitely accomplishes that goal, or whether any such claim in fact only conceals the shortcomings and perversions of revolutionary programs and of a newly established, revolutionary order. The church as a separate institution remains necessary as long as the provisional character of any established or projected political system needs articulation in order to liberate the individuals from the slavery of worshiping the perishable and provisional and—at the same time—to enable them for further changes and improvements in their own society and in the worldwide situation of mankind.

Thus the continuing existence of a religious community besides the political one and separate from it corresponds to the provisional situation of mankind in the present world, to the contrast between the ultimate destiny of man and the present form of his existence. The separate existence of the religious community, however, does not necessarily mean that religion must be a matter of private and not of public life. Since the beginnings of modern times the confessional churches have become—more or less —private associations of individual believers because their dogmatic uniformity, the intolerant claims of which had been pursued against each other in vain, offered no basis for a unified and liberal society. Therefore these confessional churches had to be turned into private associations. But on the other hand, Christianity remained a public factor in modern society and contributed to the common spirit without which even a pluralistic society cannot survive. It may even be true—as Carl Braaten suggested—that the survival of pluralism and secularity in our social system is bound up with the continuous presence of the Christian church in our society. A more pluriform but united church of the future may incorporate this public function of Christianity in modern society more convincingly than the confessional churches can do.

The church must not confine her political contribution to the witness of the provisional character of each actual form of political self-realization of man in a given society. Beyond this negative contribution, the church communicates to the individual the assurance of individual salvation in contrast with the fragmentary and provisional state of his life in the present world. But this again is not all. The church can and should articulate the political inspirations springing from this individual certainty with regard to the particular problems of a given social situation.

And further, the church can represent with her own communal life and institutional order a model and a symbol of the ultimate destiny of man in the Kingdom of God. In this Christian churches have not always succeeded, but there are examples for this highest function of the church in the society. Thus the congregational structure of some churches of the Reformation has become a model for the development of democratic political institutions. And perhaps a truly ecumenical and catholic church can become a model for the solution of that basic problem of modern society, how to reconcile pluriformity and tolerance to the fundamental requirement of a common spirit uniting the people for the sake of the public good. Such a synthesis of pluriformity and unity in a new universal church could become a symbol for peace and justice reconciling the rift and the bitterness and the opposition between individuals and races and social classes and between the nations on earth—a symbol of the Kingdom of God.